Desserts

Desserts

A cook's collection of classic recipes

consultant editor **Rosemary Wilkinson**

southwater

This edition is published by Southwater

Distributed in the UK by
The Manning Partnership
251–253 London Road East
Batheaston
Bath BA1 7RL
UK
tel. (0044) 01225 852 727
fax (0044) 01225 852 852

Distributed in Australia by
Sandstone Publishing
Unit 1, 360 Norton Street
Leichhardt
New South Wales 2040
Australia
tel. (0061) 2 9560 7888
fax (0061) 2 9560 7488

Distributed in New Zealand by
Five Mile Press NZ
PO Box 33-1071
Takapuna
Auckland 9
New Zealand
tel. (0064) 9 4444 144
fax (0064) 9 4444 518

Southwater is an imprint of Anness Publishing Limited
© 1997, 2000 Anness Publishing Limited

1 3 5 7 9 10 8 6 4 2

Publisher: Joanna Lorenz
Copy Editor: Karen Douthwaite
Designer: Bill Mason
Recipes: Carla Capalbo, Francis Cleary, Deh-Ta Hsiung, Norma MacMillan,
Laura Washburn and Stephen Wheeler
Photographers: Karl Adamson, Edward Allwright, Steve Baxter, James Duncan,
Amanda Heywood, Don Last and Michael Michaels
Food for Photography: Carla Capalbo, Francis Cleary, Carole Handslip, Jane Hartshorn,
Wendy Lee, Jane Stevenson and Elizabeth Wolf Cohen
Stylists: Carla Capalbo, Madeleine Brehaut, Diana Civil, Amanda Heywood,
Maria Kelly, Blake Minton, Kirsty Rawlings and Fiona Tillett

NOTES
For all recipes, quantities are given in both metric and imperial measures and, where appropriate, measures are also given in standard cups and spoons.
Follow one set, but not a mixture because they are not interchangeable.
Standard spoon and cup measurements are level.
1 tbsp = 15ml, 1 tsp = 5ml, 1 cup = 250ml/8fl oz
Australian standard tablespoons are 20ml. Australian readers should use 3 tsp in place of 1 tbsp for measuring small quantities of gelatine, cornflour, salt etc.
Size 3 (medium) eggs should be used unless otherwise stated.

Previously published as *Best ever Desserts*

Contents

Introduction

DESSERT RECIPES CAN RANGE from the lightest sorbet to the most substantial steamed chocolate pudding, so there are several decisions to be made when planning a menu. Your choice of what to serve will be influenced by the season and the occasion. If you are serving a filling main course you will invariably choose a light or fruity dessert to follow it, or if you plan to make a rich, creamy dessert you will deliberately pick a light main course. The time you have for preparation will also affect your choice. Many of the desserts in this selection can be made a day or two in advance, others can be started early in the day and finished off just before you eat, while frozen desserts and ice creams can be made weeks in advance, ready to serve whenever you need them. If you are planning a festive meal or entertaining a large number of people make sure you leave plenty of time for preparation, choose one of the desserts that can be made in advance and do at least some of the work for the other courses earlier in the day. That way you *and* your guests can enjoy the meal.

All the recipes have clear step-by-step instructions, so that even the traditional chef's nightmares, such as soufflés and roulades, will be easy to make and look and taste delicious. It helps to read the whole recipe through before you start, too, so that you understand the steps involved. In this introductory section you'll find special tips and techniques and some basic recipes, plus helpful hints on preparing the pastry and decorations for pies and tarts.

Black Forest Gâteau, Crème Caramel, Trifle – you will find all the old favourites here, alongside some more unusual recipes which are destined to become your new favourites. Most of the recipes are based on a family of four people, but they can easily be halved for two or doubled for eight. There are chapters on cold desserts, hot puddings, quick and easy desserts, low-calorie ideas, and many more, to make sure you serve a best-ever dessert for every occasion.

Making Shortcrust Pastry

A meltingly short, crumbly pastry sets off any filling to perfection, whether sweet or savoury. The fat content of the pastry dough can be made up of half butter or margarine and half white vegetable fat or with all one kind of fat.

INGREDIENTS

For a 23cm/9in pastry case

225g/8oz/2 cups plain flour

1.5ml/¼ tsp salt

115g/4oz/8 tbsp fat, chilled and diced

1 Sift the flour and salt into a bowl. Add the fat. Rub it into the flour with your fingertips until the mixture is crumbly.

2 Sprinkle 45ml/3 tbsp iced water over the mixture. With a fork, toss gently to mix and moisten it.

3 Press the dough into a ball. If it is too dry to hold together, gradually add another 15ml/1 tbsp iced water.

4 Wrap the ball of dough with clear film or greaseproof paper and chill it for at least 30 minutes.

5 To make pastry in a food processor: combine the flour, salt and cubed fat in the work bowl. Process, turning the machine on and off, just until the mixture is crumbly. Add 45–60ml/3–4 tbsp iced water and process again briefly – just until the dough starts to pull away from the sides of the bowl. It should still look crumbly. Remove the dough from the processor and gather it into a ball. Wrap and chill.

SHORTCRUST PASTRY VARIATIONS

For Nut Shortcrust
Add 30g/1oz/¼ cup finely chopped walnuts or pecan nuts to the flour mixture.

For Rich Shortcrust
Use 225g/8oz/2 cups flour and 175g/6oz/¾ cup fat (preferably all butter), plus 15ml/1 tbsp caster sugar if making a sweet pie. Bind with 1 egg yolk and 30–45ml/2–3 tbsp water.

For a Two-crust Pie
Increase the proportions for these pastries by 50%, thus the amounts needed for basic shortcrust pastry are: 340g/12oz/3 cups flour, 2.5ml/½ tsp salt, 175g/6oz/¾ cup fat, 75–90ml/5–6 tbsp water.

PASTRY MAKING TIPS

It helps if the fat is cold and firm, particularly if making the dough in a food processor. Cold fat has less chance of warming and softening too much when it is being rubbed into the flour, resulting in an oily pastry. Use block margarine rather than the soft tub-type for the same reason.

When rubbing the fat into the flour, if it begins to soften and feel oily, put the bowl in the fridge to chill for 20–30 minutes. Then continue to make the dough.

Liquids used should be ice-cold so that they will not soften or melt the fat.

Take care when adding the water: start with the smaller amount (added all at once, not in a dribble), and add more only if the mixture will not come together into a dough. Too much water will make the dough difficult to handle and will result in tough pastry.

When gathering the mixture together into a ball of dough, handle it as little as possible: overworked dough will again produce a tough pastry.

To avoid shrinkage, chill the pastry dough before rolling out and baking. This 'resting time' will allow any elasticity developed during mixing to relax.

Making French Flan Pastry

The pastry for tarts and flans is made with butter or margarine, giving a rich and crumbly result. The more fat used, the richer the pastry will be – almost like a biscuit dough – and the harder to roll out. If you have difficulty rolling it, you can press it into the tin instead, or roll it out between sheets of clear film. Flan pastry, like shortcrust, can be made by hand or in a food processor. Tips for making, handling and using shortcrust pastry apply equally to this type of pastry.

INGREDIENTS

For a 23cm/9in flan case

200g/7oz/1¾ cups plain flour

2.5ml/½ tsp salt

115g/4oz/½ cup butter or margarine, chilled

1 egg yolk

1.5ml/¼ tsp lemon juice

1 Sift the flour and salt into a bowl. Add the butter or margarine. Rub into the flour until the mixture resembles fine breadcrumbs.

2 In a small bowl, mix the egg yolk, lemon juice and 30ml/ 2 tbsp iced water. Add to the flour mixture. With a fork, toss gently to mix and moisten.

3 Press the dough into a rough ball. If it is too dry to come together, add 15ml/1 tbsp more water. Turn on to the work surface or a pastry board.

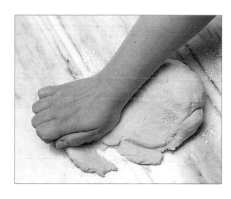

4 With the heel of your hand, push small portions of dough away from you, smearing them on the surface.

5 Continue mixing the dough in this way until it feels pliable and can easily be peeled off the work surface or pastry board.

6 Press the dough into a smooth ball. Wrap in clear film and chill for at least 30 minutes.

FLAN PASTRY VARIATIONS

For Sweet Flan Pastry
Reduce the amount of salt to 1.5ml/¼ tsp, add 15ml/1 tbsp caster sugar with the flour.

For Rich Flan Pastry
Use 200g/7oz/1¾ cups flour, 2.5ml/½ tsp salt, 150g/5oz/10 tbsp butter, 2 egg yolks and 15–30ml/ 1–2 tbsp water.

For Rich Sweet Flan Pastry
Make rich flan pastry, adding 45ml/3 tbsp caster sugar with the flour and, if liked, 2.5ml/½ tsp vanilla essence with the egg yolks.

Making Choux Pastry

Unlike other pastries, where the fat is rubbed into the flour, with choux pastry the butter is melted with water and then the flour is added, followed by eggs. The result is more of a paste than a pastry. It is easy to make, but care must be taken in measuring the ingredients.

INGREDIENTS

For 18 profiteroles or 12 éclairs

115g/4oz/½ cup butter, cut into small
   pieces

10ml/2 tsp caster sugar (optional)

1.5ml/¼ tsp salt

150g/5oz/1¼ cups plain flour

4 eggs, beaten

1 egg, beaten with 5ml/1 tsp cold water,
   for glazing

1 Preheat the oven to 220°C/
425°F/Gas 7. Combine the butter, sugar, if using, salt and 250ml/8fl oz/1 cup water in a large heavy-based saucepan. Bring to the boil over moderately high heat, stirring occasionally.

2 As soon as the mixture is boiling, remove the pan from the heat. Add the flour all at once and beat vigorously with a wooden spoon to mix the flour smoothly into the liquid.

3 Return the pan to moderate heat and cook, stirring, until the mixture forms a ball, pulling away from the side of the pan. This will take about 1 minute. Remove from the heat again and allow to cool for 3–5 minutes.

4 Add a little of the beaten eggs and beat well to incorporate. Add a little more egg and beat in well. Continue beating in the eggs until the mixture becomes a smooth and shiny paste.

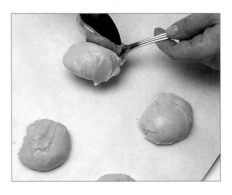

5 While still warm, shape choux puffs, éclairs, profiteroles or rings on a baking sheet lined with baking parchment.

6 Glaze with 1 egg beaten with 5ml/1 tsp cold water. Put into the preheated oven, then reduce the heat to 200°C/400°F/ Gas 6. Bake until puffed and golden brown.

SHAPING CHOUX PASTRY

For Large Puffs
Use two large spoons dipped in water. Drop the paste in 5–6cm/ 2–2½in wide blobs on the paper-lined baking sheet, leaving 4cm/1½in between each. Neaten the blobs as much as possible. Alternatively, for well-shaped puffs, pipe the paste using a piping bag fitted with a 2cm/¾in plain nozzle.

For Profiteroles
Use two small spoons or a piping bag fitted with a 1cm/½in nozzle and shape 2.5cm/1in blobs.

For Eclairs
Use a piping bag fitted with a 2cm/¾in nozzle. Pipe strips 10–13cm/4–5in long.

For a Ring
Draw a 30cm/12in circle on the paper. Spoon the paste in large blobs on the circle to make a ring. Or pipe two rings round the circle and a third on top.

BAKING TIMES FOR CHOUX PASTRY	
Large puffs and éclairs	30–35 minutes
Profiteroles	20–25 minutes
Rings	40–45 minutes

Rolling Out and Lining a Tin

A neat pastry case that doesn't distort or shrink in baking is the desired result. The key to success is handling the dough gently. Use the method here to line a round pie or tart tin that is about 5cm/2in deep.

Remove the chilled dough from the fridge and allow it to soften slightly at room temperature. Unwrap and put it on a lightly floured surface. Flatten the dough into a neat, round disc. Lightly flour the rolling pin.

1 Using even pressure, start rolling out the dough, working from the centre to the edge each time and easing the pressure slightly as you reach the edge.

2 Lift up the dough and give it a quarter turn from time to time during the rolling. This will prevent the dough sticking to the surface, and will help keep the thickness even.

3 Continue rolling out until the dough circle is about 5cm/2in larger all round than the tin. It should be about 3mm/⅛in thick.

4 Set the rolling pin on the dough, near one side of the circle. Fold the outside edge of the dough over the pin, then roll the pin over the dough to wrap the dough round it. Do this gently and loosely.

5 Hold the pin over the tin and gently unroll the dough so it drapes into the tin, centring it as much as possible.

6 With your fingertips, lift and ease the dough into the tin, gently pressing it over the bottom and up the side. Turn excess dough over the rim and trim it with a knife or scissors, depending on the edge to be made.

Finishing the Edge

1 *For a forked edge:* trim the dough even with the rim and press it flat. Firmly and evenly press the prongs of a fork all round the edge. If the fork sticks, dip it in flour every so often.

2 *For a crimped edge:* trim the dough to leave an overhang of about 1.5cm/½in all round. Fold the extra dough under. Put the knuckle or tip of the index finger of one of your hands inside the edge, pointing directly out. With the thumb and index finger of your other hand, pinch the dough edge around your index finger into a "V" shape. Continue all the way round the edge.

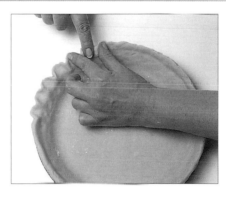

3 *For a ruffled edge:* trim the dough to leave an overhang of about 1.5cm/½in all round. Fold the extra dough under. Hold the thumb and index finger of one of your hands about 2.5cm/1in apart, inside the edge, pointing directly out. With the index finger of your other hand, gently pull the dough between them, to the end of the rim. Continue this all the way round the edge.

4 *For a cutout edge:* trim the dough even with the rim and press it flat on the rim. With a small pastry cutter, cut out decorative shapes from the dough trimmings. Moisten the edge of the pastry case and press the cutouts in place, overlapping them slightly if you like.

5 *For a ribbon edge:* trim the dough even with the rim and press it flat. Cut long strips about 2cm/¾in wide from the dough trimmings. Moisten the edge and press one end of a strip on to it. Twist the strip gently and press it on to the edge again. Continue all the way round the edge.

Preparing Fresh Fruit

PEELING AND TRIMMING FRUIT

Citrus Fruit

To peel completely: cut a slice from the top and from the base. Set the fruit base down on a work surface. Using a small sharp knife, cut off the peel lengthways in thick strips. Remove the coloured rind and all the white pith (which has a bitter taste). Cut, following the curve of the fruit.

To remove rind: use a vegetable peeler to shave off the rind in wide strips, taking none of the white pith. Use these strips whole or cut them into fine shreds with a sharp knife, according to recipe directions. Or rub the fruit against the fine holes of a metal grater, turning the fruit so you take just the coloured rind and not the white pith. Or use a special tool, called a citrus zester, to take fine threads of rind. (Finely chop the threads as an alternative method to grating.)

Kiwi fruit

Follow the citrus fruit technique, taking off the peel in thin lengthways strips.

Apples, pears, quinces, mangoes, papayas

Use a small sharp knife or a vegetable peeler. Take off the peel in long strips, as thinly as possible.

Peaches, apricots

Cut a cross in the base. Immerse the fruit in boiling water. Leave for 10–30 seconds (according to ripeness), then drain and immerse in iced water. The skin should slip off easily.

Pineapple

Cut off the leafy crown. Cut a slice from the base and set the pineapple upright. With a sharp knife, cut off the peel lengthways, cutting thickly to remove the brown "eyes" with it.

Bananas, lychees, avocados

Make a small cut and remove the peel with your fingers or a knife.

Passion fruit, pomegranates

Cut in half, or cut a slice off the top. With a spoon, scoop the flesh and seeds into a bowl.

Star fruit (carambola)

Trim off the tough, darkened edges of the five segments.

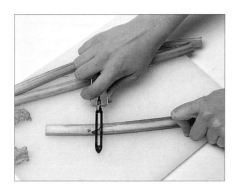

Rhubarb

Cut off the leaves and discard them (they are poisonous). Peel off any tough skin.

Fresh currants (red, black, white)

Pull each cluster through the prongs of a fork to remove the currants from the stalks.

Fresh dates

Squeeze gently at the stalk end to remove the rather tough skin.

CORING AND STONING OR SEEDING FRUIT

Apples, pears, quinces

For whole fruit: use an apple corer to stamp out the whole core from stalk end to base. Alternatively, working up from the base, use a melon baller to cut out the core. Leave the stalk end intact.

For halves: use a melon baller to scoop out the core. Cut out the stalk and base using a small sharp knife.
For quarters: cut out the stalk and core with a serrated knife.

Citrus fruit

With the tip of a pointed knife, nick out pips from slices or segments.

Cherries

Use a cherry stoner to achieve the neatest results.

Peaches, apricots, nectarines, plums

Cut the fruit in half, cutting round the indentation. Twist the halves apart. Lift out the stone, or lever it out with the tip of a sharp knife.

Fresh dates

Cut the fruit lengthways in half and lift out the stone. Or, if the fruit is to be used whole, cut in from the stalk end with a thin bladed knife to loosen the stone, then remove it.

Apples, quinces

For rings: remove the core and seeds with an apple corer. Set the fruit on its side and cut across into thick or thin rings, as required.

For slices: cut the fruit in half and remove core and seeds with a melon baller. Set one half cut side down and cut it across into neat slices, thick or thin according to recipe directions. Or cut the fruit into quarters and remove core and seeds with a knife. Cut lengthways into neat slices.

Mangoes

Cut lengthways on either side of the large flat stone in the centre. Curve the cut slightly to follow the shape of the stone. Cut the flesh from the two thin ends of the stone.

Grapes

Cut the fruit lengthways in half. Use a small knife to nick out the pips. Alternatively, use the curved end of a sterilized hair grip.

Papayas, melons

Cut the fruit in half. Scoop out the seeds from the central hollow, then scrape away any fibres.

Star fruit (carambola), watermelon

With the tip of a pointed knife, nick out pips from slices.

Pineapple

For spears and wedges: cut out the core neatly with a sharp knife.
For rings: cut out the core with a small pastry cutter.

Gooseberries

Use scissors to trim off the stalk and flower ends.

Strawberries

Use a special huller to remove leafy green top and central core. Or cut these out with a small sharp knife.

Avocado

Cut the fruit in half lengthways. Stick the tip of a sharp knife into the stone and lever it out without damaging the surrounding flesh.

Pears

For fans: cut the fruit in half and remove the core and seeds with a melon baller. Set one half cut side down and cut lengthways into thin slices, not cutting all the way through at the stalk end. Gently fan out the slices so they are overlapping each other evenly. Transfer the pear fan to plate or pastry case using a palette knife.
For slices: follow apple technique.

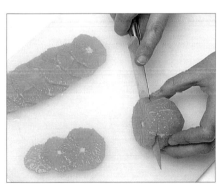

Citrus fruit

For slices: using a serrated knife, cut the fruit across into neat slices.

For segments: hold the peeled fruit in your cupped palm, over a bowl to catch the juice. Working from the side of the fruit to the centre, slide the knife down one side of a separating membrane to free the flesh from it. Then slide the knife down the other side of that segment to free it from the membrane there. Drop the segment into the bowl. Continue cutting out the segments, folding back the membrane like the pages of a book as you work. When all the segments have been cut out, squeeze all the juice from the membrane.

Peaches, nectarines, apricots, plums

For slices: follow apple technique.

Papayas, avocados

For slices: follow apple technique. Or cut the unpeeled fruit into wedges, removing the central seeds or stone. Set each wedge peel side down and slide the knife down the length to cut the flesh away from the peel.
For fans: follow pear technique.

Melon

For slices: follow papaya technique.
For balls: Use a melon baller.

Mangoes

Cut the peeled flesh into slices or cubes, according to recipe directions.

Pineapple

For spears: cut the peeled fruit lengthways in half and then into quarters. Cut each quarter into spears and cut out the core.
For chunks: cut the peeled fruit into spears. Remove the core. Cut across each spear into chunks.
For rings: cut the peeled fruit across into slices. Stamp out the central core from each slice using a pastry cutter.

Kiwi fruit, star fruit (carambola)

Cut the fruit across into neat slices; discard the ends.

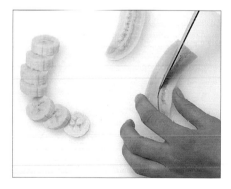

Banana

Cut the fruit across into neat slices. Or cut in half and then lengthways into quarters.

Gelatine

DISSOLVING GELATINE

It's important to dissolve gelatine correctly, or it can spoil the texture and set of your finished dessert.

1 Place 45ml/3 tbsp very hot water per sachet of gelatine in a small bowl.

2 Sprinkle the gelatine over the liquid. Always add the gelatine to the liquid, never the other way round.

3 Stir briskly until the gelatine is completely dissolved. There should be no visible crystals and the liquid should be clear. If necessary, stand the container in a pan of hot water over a low heat until dissolved. Do not allow the gelatine to boil.

VEGETARIAN ALTERNATIVE

There is a vegetarian alternative to gelatine, which can be used in the appropriate recipes, if you wish. Follow the instructions on the packet, but in general you should sprinkle the alternative on to cold liquids and stir until completely dissolved. Next, heat the mixture to near boiling. (If setting proves difficult add more of the gelatine alternative to the mixture and reheat.) It is now ready to be used as specified in the recipe, but should be allowed to set for about 1 hour, or until firm and should always be allowed to cool.

Redcurrant and Raspberry Coulis

A dessert sauce for the height of summer to serve with light meringues and fruit sorbets. Make it particularly pretty with a decoration of fresh flowers and leaves.

INGREDIENTS

Serves 6

225g/8oz/2 cups redcurrants
450g/1lb/2⅔ cups raspberries
50g/2oz/½ cup icing sugar
15ml/1 tbsp cornflour
juice of 1 orange
30ml/2 tbsp double cream, to decorate

1 Strip the redcurrants from their stalks using a fork. Place in a food processor or blender with the raspberries and sugar, and purée until smooth.

2 Press the mixture through a fine sieve into a bowl and discard the seeds and pulp.

3 Blend the cornflour with the orange juice then stir into the fruit purée. Transfer to a saucepan and bring to the boil, stirring continuously, and cook for 1–2 minutes until smooth and thick. Leave until cold.

4 Spoon the sauce over each plate. Drip the cream from a teaspoon to make small dots evenly round the edge. Draw a cocktail stick through the dots to form heart shapes. Place the meringue or scoop sorbet into the middle and decorate with flowers.

Crème Anglaise

Here is the classic English custard, light, creamy and delicious – far superior to packet versions. Serve hot or cold.

INGREDIENTS

Serves 4

1 vanilla pod
450ml/¾ pint/1⅞ cups milk
40g/1½oz/3 tbsp caster sugar
4 egg yolks

1 Split the vanilla pod and place in a saucepan with the milk. Bring slowly to the boil. Remove from the heat, then cover and infuse for 10 minutes before removing the pod.

2 Beat together the sugar and egg yolks until thick, light and creamy.

3 Slowly pour the warm milk on to the egg mixture, stirring constantly.

4 Transfer to the top of a double boiler or place the bowl over a saucepan of hot water. Stir constantly over a low heat for 10 minutes or until the mixture coats the back of the spoon. Remove from the heat immediately as curdling will occur if the custard is allowed to simmer.

5 Strain the custard into a jug if serving hot or, if serving cold, strain into a bowl and cover the surface with buttered paper or clear film.

VARIATION

Infuse a few strips of thinly pared lemon or orange rind with the milk, instead of the vanilla pod.

Sabayon

Serve this frothy sauce hot over steamed puddings or chill and serve just as it is with light dessert biscuits or whatever you prefer. Never let it stand for any length of time, as it will collapse.

INGREDIENTS

Serves 4-6

1 egg
2 egg yolks
75g/3oz/⅔ cup caster sugar
150ml/¼ pint/⅔ cup sweet white wine
finely grated rind and juice of 1 lemon

1 Whisk the egg, yolks and sugar until they are pale and thick.

2 Stand the bowl over a saucepan of hot – not boiling – water. Add the wine and lemon juice, a little at a time, whisking vigorously.

3 Continue whisking until the mixture is thick enough to leave a trail. Whisk in the lemon rind. If serving hot, pour immediately over pudding or fruit salad.

4 To serve cold, place over a bowl of iced water and whisk until chilled. Pour into small glasses and serve at once.

Butterscotch Sauce

A deliciously sweet sauce which will be loved by adults and children alike! Serve with ice cream and pancakes or waffles.

INGREDIENTS

Serves 4–6

75g/3oz/6 tbsp butter

175g/6oz/¾ cup soft dark brown sugar

175ml/6fl oz/¾ cup evaporated milk

50g/2oz/½ cup hazelnuts

1 Melt the butter and sugar in a heavy-based pan, bring to the boil and boil for 2 minutes. Cool for 5 minutes.

2 Heat the evaporated milk to just below boiling point, then gradually stir into the sugar mixture. Cook over a low heat for 2 minutes, stirring frequently.

3 Spread the hazelnuts on a baking sheet and toast under a hot grill.

4 Tip the nuts on to a clean dish towel and rub them briskly to remove the skins.

5 Chop the nuts roughly and stir into the sauce. Serve hot, poured over scoops of vanilla ice cream and warm waffles or pancakes.

Brandy Butter

This is traditionally served with Christmas pudding and mince pies but a good spoonful on a hot baked apple is equally delicious.

INGREDIENTS

Serves 6

100g/4oz/½ cup butter

100g/4oz/½ cup icing, caster or soft light brown sugar

45ml/3 tbsp brandy

1 Cream the butter until very pale and soft. Beat in the sugar gradually.

2 Add the brandy, a few drops at a time, beating continuously. Add enough for a good flavour, but take care that the mixture does not curdle.

3 Pile into a small serving dish and allow to harden. Alternatively, spread on to aluminium foil and chill until firm. Cut into shapes with small fancy cutters.

VARIATION

Cumberland Rum Butter
Use soft light brown sugar and rum instead of brandy. Beat in the grated rind of 1 orange and a good pinch of mixed spice with the sugar.

Chocolate Fudge Sauce

A real treat if you're not counting calories. Fabulous with scoops of vanilla ice cream.

INGREDIENTS

Serves 6

150ml/¼ pint/⅔ cup double cream
50g/2oz/4 tbsp butter
50g/2oz/¼ cup granulated sugar
175g/6oz plain chocolate
30ml/2 tbsp brandy

VARIATIONS

White Chocolate and Orange Sauce:
40g/1½oz/3 tbsp caster sugar, to replace granulated sugar
finely grated rind of 1 orange
175g/6oz white chocolate, to replace plain chocolate
30ml/2 tbsp orange liqueur, to replace brandy

Coffee Chocolate Fudge:
50g/2oz/¼ cup light brown sugar, to replace granulated sugar
30ml/2 tbsp coffee liqueur or dark rum, to replace brandy
15ml/1 tbsp coffee essence

1 Heat the cream with the butter and sugar in the top of a double boiler or in a heatproof bowl over a saucepan of hot water. Stir until smooth, then cool.

2 Break the chocolate into the cream. Stir until it is melted and thoroughly combined.

3 Stir in the brandy a little at a time, then cool to room temperature.

4 For the White Chocolate and Orange Sauce, heat the cream and butter with the sugar and orange rind in the top of a double boiler, until dissolved. Then, follow the recipe to the end, but using white chocolate and orange liqueur instead.

5 For the Coffee Chocolate Fudge, follow the recipe, using light brown sugar and coffee liqueur or rum. Stir in the coffee essence at the end.

6 Serve the sauce over cream-filled profiteroles, and serve any that is left over separately.

Glossy Chocolate Sauce

Delicious poured over ice cream or on hot or cold desserts, this sauce also freezes well. Pour into a freezer-proof container, seal, and keep for up to three months. Thaw at room temperature.

INGREDIENTS

Serves 6

115g/4oz/½ cup caster sugar
175g/6oz plain chocolate, broken into squares
30ml/2 tbsp unsalted butter
30ml/2 tbsp brandy or orange juice

1 Place the sugar and 60ml/4 tbsp of water in a saucepan and heat gently, stirring occasionally, until the sugar has dissolved.

2 Stir in the chocolate, a few squares at a time, until melted, then add the butter in the same way. Do not allow the sauce to boil. Stir in the brandy or orange juice and serve warm.

COLD DESSERTS

Boodles Orange Fool

This fool became the speciality of Boodles Club, a gentlemen's club in London's St James's.

Serves 4

4 trifle sponge cakes, cubed

300ml/½ pint/1¼ cups double cream

30–60ml/2–4 tbsp caster sugar

grated rind and juice of 2 oranges

grated rind and juice of 1 lemon

orange and lemon slices and rind,
  to decorate

1 Line the base and halfway up the sides of a large glass serving bowl or china dish with the cubed trifle sponge cakes.

2 Whip the cream with the sugar until it starts to thicken, then gradually whip in the fruit juices, adding the fruit rinds once most of the juices have been incorporated.

3 Carefully pour the cream mixture into the bowl or dish, taking care not to dislodge the sponge. Cover and chill for 3–4 hours. Serve decorated with orange and lemon slices and rind.

Apricot and Orange Jelly

A light and refreshing dessert for a summer's day.

Serves 4

350g/12oz well-flavoured fresh ripe
  apricots, stoned

50–75g/2–3oz/about ⅓ cup
  granulated sugar

about 300ml/½ pint/1¼ cups freshly
  squeezed orange juice

15ml/1 tbsp powdered gelatine

single cream, to serve

finely chopped candied orange peel,
  to decorate

1 Heat the apricots, sugar and 120ml/4fl oz/½ cup of the orange juice, stirring until the sugar has dissolved. Simmer gently until the apricots are tender.

2 Press the apricot mixture through a nylon sieve into a small measuring jug using a spoon.

3 Pour 45ml/3 tbsp of the orange juice into a small heatproof bowl, sprinkle over the gelatine and leave for about 5 minutes, until softened.

4 Place the bowl over a saucepan of hot water and heat until the gelatine has dissolved. Slowly pour into the apricot mixture, stirring all the time. Make up to 600ml/ 1 pint/2½ cups with the remaining orange juice.

5 Pour the apricot mixture into four individual dishes and chill until set. To serve, pour a thin layer of cream over the surface, and decorate with candied orange peel.

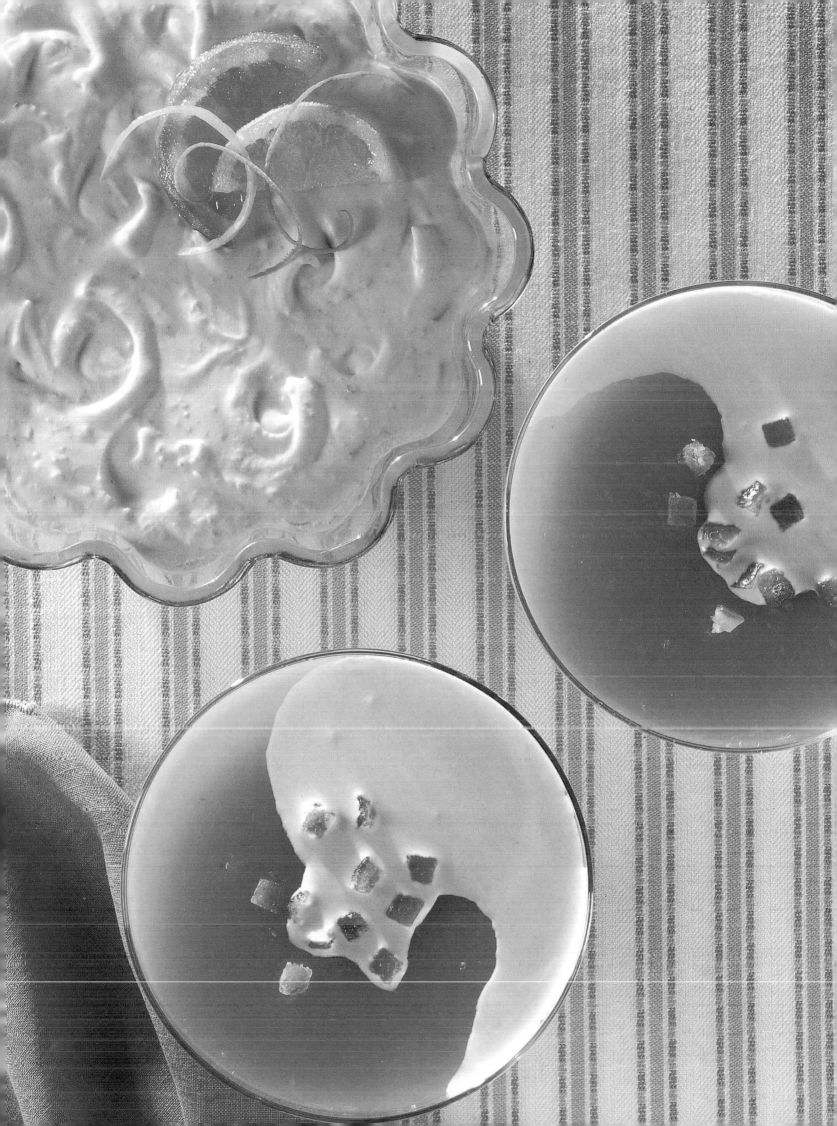

Tangerine Trifle

An unusual variation on a traditional trifle – of course, you can add a little alcohol if you wish.

INGREDIENTS

Serves 4

5 trifle sponges, halved lengthways

30ml/2 tbsp apricot jam

15–20 ratafia biscuits

142g/4¾oz packet tangerine jelly

300g/11oz can mandarin oranges, drained, reserving juice

600ml/1 pint/2½ cups ready-made (or home-made) custard

whipped cream and shreds of orange rind, to decorate

caster sugar, for sprinkling

1 Spread the halved sponge cakes with apricot jam and arrange in the base of a deep serving bowl or glass dish. Sprinkle over the ratafia biscuits.

2 Break up the jelly into a heatproof measuring jug, add the juice from the canned mandarins and dissolve in a pan of hot water or in the microwave. Stir until the liquid clears.

3 Make up to 600ml/1 pint/ 2½ cups with ice cold water, stir well and leave to cool for up to 30 minutes. Scatter the mandarin oranges over the cakes and ratafias.

4 Pour the jelly over the mandarin oranges, cake and ratafias and chill for 1 hour.

5 When the jelly has set, pour the custard smoothly over the top and chill again.

6 When ready to serve, pipe the whipped cream over the custard. Wash the orange rind shreds, sprinkle them with caster sugar and use to decorate the trifle.

Lemon Soufflé with Blackberries

The simple fresh taste of cold lemon soufflé combines well with rich blackberry sauce, and the colour contrast looks wonderful, too. Blueberries or raspberries make equally delicious alternatives to blackberries.

Serves 6

grated rind of 1 lemon and juice of 2
   lemons
15ml/1 tbsp/1 sachet powdered gelatine
5 small eggs, separated
150g/5oz/¾ cup caster sugar
few drops vanilla essence
400ml/14fl oz/1⅔ cups whipping cream

For the sauce
175g/6oz/¾ cup blackberries (fresh or
   frozen)
30–45ml/2–3 tbsp caster sugar
few fresh blackberries and blackberry
   leaves, to decorate

1 Place the lemon juice in a small pan and heat through. Sprinkle on the gelatine and leave to dissolve or heat further until clear. Allow to cool.

2 Put the lemon rind, egg yolks, sugar and vanilla into a large bowl and whisk until the mixture is very thick, pale and creamy.

3 Whisk the egg whites until stiff and almost peaky. Whip the cream until stiff.

4 Stir the gelatine mixture into the yolks, then fold in the whipped cream and lastly the egg whites. Turn into a 1.5 litre/ 2½ pint/6 cup soufflé dish and freeze for about 2 hours.

5 To make the sauce, place the blackberries in a pan with the sugar and cook for 4–6 minutes, until the juices begin to run and all the sugar has dissolved. Pass through a sieve to remove the seeds, then chill.

6 When the soufflé is almost frozen, but still spoonable, scoop or spoon out on to individual plates and serve with the blackberry sauce, decorated with fresh blackberries and blackberry leaves.

Chocolate Mandarin Trifle

Trifle is always a tempting treat, but when a rich chocolate and mascarpone custard is combined with amaretto and mandarin oranges, it becomes irresistible.

INGREDIENTS

Serves 6–8

4 trifle sponges

14 amaretti biscuits

60ml/4 tbsp Amaretto di Saronno or sweet
   sherry

8 mandarin oranges

For the custard

200g/7oz plain chocolate, broken into
   squares

30ml/2 tbsp cornflour or custard powder

30ml/2 tbsp caster sugar

2 egg yolks

200ml/7fl oz/⅞ cup milk

250g/9oz/generous 1 cup mascarpone
   cheese

For the topping

250g/9oz/generous 1 cup fromage frais

chocolate shapes

mandarin slices

1 Break up the trifle sponges and place them in a large glass serving dish. Crumble the amaretti biscuits over and then sprinkle with amaretto or sweet sherry.

2 Squeeze the juice from 2 of the mandarins and sprinkle into the dish. Segment the rest and put in the dish.

3 Make the custard. Melt the chocolate in a heatproof bowl over hot water. In a separate bowl, mix the cornflour or custard powder, sugar and egg yolks to a smooth paste.

4 Heat the milk in a small saucepan until almost boiling, then pour in a steady stream on to the egg yolk mixture, stirring constantly. Return to the clean pan and stir over a low heat until the custard has thickened slightly and is smooth.

5 Stir the mascarpone until melted, then add the melted chocolate, mixing it thoroughly. Spread evenly over the trifle, cool, then chill until set.

6 To finish, spread the fromage frais over the custard, then decorate with chocolate shapes and the remaining mandarin slices just before serving.

COOK'S TIP

Always use the best chocolate which has a high percentage of cocoa solids, and take care not to overheat the chocolate when melting as it will lose its gloss and look "grainy".

Lime Sherbet

This light, refreshing sherbet is a good dessert to serve after a substantial main course.

INGREDIENTS

Serves 4

250g/9oz/1¼ cups granulated sugar
grated rind of 1 lime
175ml/6fl oz/¾ cup freshly squeezed lime
  juice
15–30ml/1–2 tbsp fresh lemon juice
icing sugar, to taste
slivers of lime rind, to decorate

1 In a small heavy saucepan, dissolve the granulated sugar in 600ml/1 pint/2½ cups water, without stirring, over medium heat. When the sugar has dissolved, boil for 5–6 minutes. Remove from the heat and let cool.

2 Combine the cooled sugar syrup and lime rind and juice in a measuring jug or bowl. Stir well. Taste and adjust the flavour by adding lemon juice or some icing sugar, if necessary. Do not over-sweeten.

3 Freeze the mixture in an ice-cream maker, following the manufacturer's instructions.

4 If you do not have an ice-cream maker, pour the mixture into a metal or plastic freezer container and freeze until softly set, about 3 hours.

5 Remove from the container and chop roughly into 7.5cm/3in pieces. Place in a food processor and process until smooth. Return the mixture to the freezer container and freeze again until set. Repeat this freezing and chopping process two or three times, until a smooth consistency is obtained.

6 Serve in scoops decorated with slivers of lime rind.

COOK'S TIP

If using an ice-cream maker for these sherbets, check the manufacturer's instructions to find out the freezing capacity. If necessary, halve the recipe quantities.

Gooseberry and Elderflower Cream

When elderflowers are in season, instead of using the cordial, cook two to three elderflower heads with the gooseberries.

Serves 4

500g/1¼lb gooseberries, topped and
  tailed
300ml/½ pint/1¼ cups double cream
about 115g/4oz/1 cup icing sugar, to taste
30ml/2 tbsp elderflower cordial or orange
  flower water (optional)
mint sprigs, to decorate
almond biscuits, to serve

2 Beat the cream until soft peaks form, then fold in half the gooseberries. Sweeten and add elderflower cordial or orange flower water, if using. Sweeten the remaining gooseberries.

3 Layer the cream mixture and the crushed gooseberries in four dessert dishes or tall glasses, then cover and chill. Decorate with mint sprigs and serve accompanied by almond biscuits.

1 Place the gooseberries in a heavy saucepan, cover and cook over a low heat, shaking the pan occasionally, until the gooseberries are tender. Tip the gooseberries into a bowl, crush them, then leave to cool completely.

COOK'S TIP

If preferred, the cooked gooseberries can be puréed and sieved. An equivalent quantity of real custard can replace the cream.

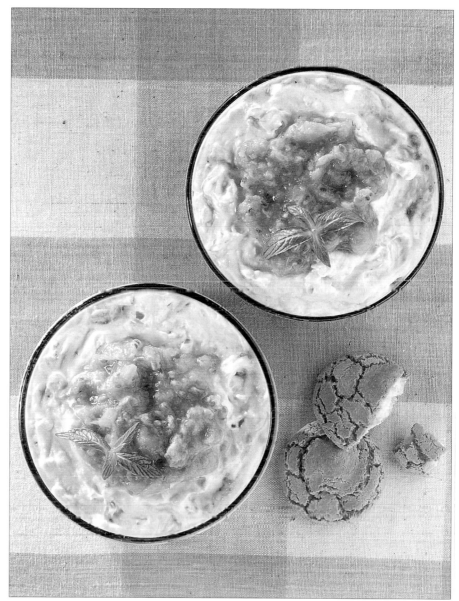

Apricots with Orange Cream

Mascarpone is a very rich cream cheese made from thick Lombardy cream. It is delicious flavoured with orange as a topping for these poached, chilled apricots.

INGREDIENTS

Serves 4

450g/1lb/2 cups ready-to-eat dried apricots

strip of orange peel

1 cinnamon stick

45ml/3 tbsp caster sugar

150ml/¼ pint/⅔ cup sweet dessert wine (such as Muscat de Beaumes de Venise)

115g/4oz/½ cup mascarpone cheese

45ml/3 tbsp orange juice

pinch of ground cinnamon and fresh mint sprig, to decorate

1 Place the apricots, orange peel, cinnamon stick and 15ml/ 1 tbsp of the sugar in a pan and cover with 450ml/¼ pint/1⅞ cups cold water. Bring to the boil, cover and simmer gently for 25 minutes, until the fruit is tender.

2 Remove from the heat and stir in the dessert wine. Leave until cold, then chill for at least 3–4 hours or overnight.

3 Mix together the mascarpone cheese, orange juice and the remaining sugar in a bowl and beat well until smooth, then chill.

4 Just before serving remove the cinnamon stick and orange peel and serve with a spoonful of the orange cream sprinkled with cinnamon and decorated with a sprig of fresh mint.

Rhubarb and Orange Fool

Perhaps this traditional English pudding got its name because it is so easy to make that even a "fool" can attempt it.

INGREDIENTS

Serves 4

30ml/2 tbsp orange juice

5ml/1 tsp finely shredded orange rind

1kg/2lb (about 10–12 stems) rhubarb, chopped

15ml/1 tbsp redcurrant jelly

45ml/3 tbsp caster sugar

150g/5oz/⅔ cup ready-to-serve thick and creamy custard

150ml/¼ pint/⅔ cup double cream, whipped

sweet biscuits, to serve

1 Place the orange juice and rind, the rhubarb, redcurrant jelly and sugar in a saucepan. Cover and simmer gently for about 8 minutes, stirring occasionally, until the rhubarb is just tender but not mushy.

2 Remove the pan from the heat, transfer the rhubarb to a bowl and leave to cool completely.

3 Drain the cooled rhubarb to remove some of the liquid. Reserve a few pieces of the rhubarb and a little orange rind for decoration. Purée the remaining rhubarb in a food processor or blender, or push through a sieve.

4 Stir the custard into the purée, then fold in the whipped cream. Spoon the fool into individual bowls, cover and chill. Just before serving, top with the reserved fruit and rind. Serve with crisp, sweet biscuits.

Cherry Syllabub

This recipe follows the style of the earliest syllabubs from the sixteenth and seventeenth centuries, producing a frothy, creamy layer over a liquid one.

Serves 4

225g/8oz ripe dark cherries, stoned and
    chopped
30ml/2 tbsp kirsch
2 egg whites
75g/3oz/scant ½ cup caster sugar
30ml/2 tbsp lemon juice
150ml/¼ pint/⅔ cup sweet white wine
300ml/½ pint/1¼ cups double cream

1 Divide the chopped cherries among six tall dessert glasses and sprinkle over the kirsch.

2 In a clean bowl, whisk the egg whites until stiff. Gently fold in the sugar, lemon juice and wine.

3 In a separate bowl (but using the same whisk), lightly beat the cream then fold into the egg white mixture.

4 Spoon the cream mixture over the cherries, then chill overnight.

Rose Petal Cream

This is an old-fashioned junket which is set with rennet – don't move it while it is setting, otherwise it will separate.

Serves 4

600ml/1 pint/2½ cups milk
45ml/3 tbsp caster sugar
several drops triple-strength rosewater
10ml/2 tsp rennet
60ml/4 tbsp double cream
sugared rose petals, to decorate (optional)

1 Gently heat the milk and 30ml/2 tbsp of the sugar, stirring continuously, until the sugar has melted and the temperature reaches 36.9° C/98.4°F, or the milk feels lukewarm.

2 Stir rosewater to taste into the milk, then remove the pan from the heat before stirring in the rennet.

3 Pour the milk into a serving dish and leave undisturbed for 2–3 hours, until the junket has set.

4 Stir the remaining sugar into the cream, then carefully spoon over the junket. Decorate with sugared rose petals, if you like.

COOK'S TIP

Only use rose petals taken from bushes which have not been sprayed with chemicals of any kind.

Raspberry Meringue Gâteau

A rich, hazelnut meringue sandwiched with whipped cream and raspberries makes an irresistible dessert for a special occasion.

INGREDIENTS

Serves 6
4 egg whites
225g/8oz/1 cup caster sugar
a few drops of vanilla essence
5ml/1 tsp distilled malt vinegar
115g/4oz/1 cup roasted and chopped
   hazelnuts, ground
300ml/½ pint/1¼ cups double cream
350g/12oz/2 cups raspberries
icing sugar, for dusting
mint sprigs, to decorate

For the sauce
225g/8oz/1⅓ cups raspberries
45–60ml/3–4 tbsp icing sugar, sifted
15ml/1 tbsp orange liqueur

1 Preheat the oven to 180°C/ 350°F/Gas 4. Grease two 20cm/8in sandwich tins and line the bases with greaseproof paper.

2 Whisk the egg whites in a large bowl until they hold stiff peaks, then gradually whisk in the caster sugar a tablespoon at a time, whisking well after each addition.

COOK'S TIP
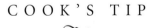

You can buy roasted chopped hazelnuts in supermarkets. Otherwise toast whole hazelnuts under the grill and rub off the flaky skins using a clean dish towel. To chop finely, process in a blender or food processor for a few moments.

3 Continue whisking the meringue mixture for a minute of two until very stiff, then fold in the vanilla essence, vinegar and ground hazelnuts.

4 Divide the meringue mixture between the prepared sandwich tins and spread level. Bake for 50–60 minutes, until crisp. Remove the meringues from the tins and leave them to cool on a wire rack.

5 While the meringues are cooling, make the sauce. Process the raspberries with the icing sugar and orange liqueur in a blender or food processor, then press the purée through a fine nylon sieve to remove any pips. Chill the sauce until ready to serve.

6 Whip the cream until it forms soft peaks, then gently fold in the raspberries. Sandwich the meringue rounds together with the raspberry cream.

7 Dust the top of the gâteau with icing sugar. Decorate with mint sprigs and serve with the raspberry sauce.

VARIATION

Fresh redcurrants make a good alternative to raspberries. Pick over the fruit, then pull each sprig gently through the prongs of a fork to release the redcurrants. Add them to the whipped cream with a little icing sugar, to taste.

Creole Ambrosia

A refreshing cold fruity pudding that can be made at any time of the year.

Serves 6

6 oranges

1 coconut

25g/1oz/2 tbsp caster sugar

1 Peel the oranges removing all white pith, then slice thinly, picking out seeds with the point of a knife. Do this on a plate to catch the juice.

2 Pierce the "eyes" of the coconut and pour away the milk, then crack open the coconut with a hammer. (This is best done outside on a stone surface.)

> ### COOK'S TIP
>
> Mangoes instead of oranges make the dessert more exotic but less authentically Creole.

3 Peel the coconut with a sharp knife, then grate half the flesh coarsely, either on a hand grater or on the grating blade of a blender or food processor.

4 Layer the coconut and orange slices in a glass bowl, starting and finishing with the coconut. After each orange layer, sprinkle on a little sugar and pour over some of the reserved orange juice.

5 Let the dessert stand for 2 hours before serving, either at room temperature or, in hot weather, keep it refrigerated.

Watermelon Sherbet

A pretty pink sherbet that makes a light and refreshing dessert, or that could be served before the main course to cleanse the palate at a grand dinner.

INGREDIENTS

Serves 6

1kg/2¼lb piece watermelon

200g/7oz/1 cup caster sugar

juice of 1 lemon

2 egg whites

mint leaves, to decorate

1 Cut the watermelon in wedges, then cut it away from the rind, cubing the flesh and picking out all the seeds.

2 Purée three-quarters of the flesh in a food processor or blender, but mash the last quarter on a plate – this will give the sherbet more texture.

3 Stir the sugar with the lemon juice and 120ml/4fl oz/½ cup cold water in a saucepan over very low heat until the sugar dissolves and the syrup clears.

4 Mix all the watermelon and the syrup in a large bowl and transfer to a freezer container.

5 Freeze for 1–1½ hours, until the edges begin to set. Beat the mixture, return to the freezer and freeze for a further 1 hour.

6 When the hour is up, whisk the egg whites to soft peaks. Beat the iced mixture again and fold in the egg whites. Return to the freezer for a further 1 hour, then beat once more and freeze firm.

7 Transfer the sherbet from the freezer to the fridge for 20–30 minutes before it is to be served. Serve in scoops, decorated with mint leaves.

Coffee, Vanilla and Chocolate Stripe

This looks really special served in elegant wine glasses and tastes appropriately exquisite.

INGREDIENTS

Serves 6

285g/10½oz/1½ cups caster sugar

90ml/6 tbsp cornflour

900ml/1½ pints/3¾ cups milk

3 egg yolks

75g/3oz/6 tbsp unsalted butter, at room temperature

20ml/generous 1 tbsp instant coffee powder

10ml/2 tsp vanilla essence

30ml/2 tbsp cocoa powder

whipped cream, to serve

1 To make the coffee layer, place 90g/3½oz/½ cup of the sugar and 30ml/2 tbsp of the cornflour in a heavy-based saucepan. Gradually add one-third of the milk, whisking until well blended. Over a medium heat, whisk in one of the egg yolks and bring to the boil, whisking. Boil for 1 minute.

2 Remove the pan from the heat. Stir in 25g/1oz/2 tbsp of the butter and the instant coffee powder. Set aside in the pan to cool slightly.

3 Divide the coffee mixture among six wine glasses. Smooth the tops before the mixture sets.

4 Wipe any dribbles on the insides and outsides of the glasses with damp kitchen paper.

5 To make the vanilla layer, place half of the remaining sugar and cornflour in a heavy-based saucepan. Whisk in 300ml/½ pint/1¼ cups of the milk. Over a medium heat, whisk in another egg yolk and bring to the boil, whisking. Boil for 1 minute.

6 Remove the pan from the heat and stir in 25g/1oz/2 tbsp of the butter and the vanilla. Leave to cool slightly, then spoon into the glasses on top of the coffee layer. Smooth the tops and wipe the glasses with kitchen paper.

7 To make the chocolate layer, place the remaining sugar and cornflour in a heavy-based saucepan. Gradually whisk in the remaining milk and continue whisking until blended. Over a medium heat, whisk in the last egg yolk and bring to the boil, whisking constantly. Boil for 1 minute. Remove from the heat, stir in the remaining butter and the cocoa. Leave to cool slightly, then spoon into the glasses on top of the vanilla layer. Chill until set.

8 Pipe swirls of whipped cream on top of each dessert just before serving.

COOK'S TIP

For a special occasion, prepare the vanilla layer using a fresh vanilla pod. Choose a plump, supple pod and split it down the centre with a sharp knife. Add to the mixture with the milk and discard the pod before spooning the mixture into the glasses. The flavour will be more pronounced and the pudding will have pretty brown speckles from the vanilla seeds.

Chocolate Hazelnut Galettes

Chocolate rounds sandwiched with fromage frais. If only all sandwiches looked and tasted this good.

INGREDIENTS

Serves 4

175g/6oz plain chocolate, broken into squares
45ml/3 tbsp single cream
30ml/2 tbsp flaked hazelnuts
115g/4oz white chocolate, broken into squares
175g/6oz/¾ cup fromage frais (8% fat)
15ml/1 tbsp dry sherry
60ml/4 tbsp finely chopped hazelnuts, toasted
physalis (Cape gooseberries), dipped in white chocolate, to decorate

1 Melt the plain chocolate in a heatproof bowl over hot water, then remove from the heat and stir in the cream.

2 Draw 12 x 7.5cm/3in circles on sheets of non-stick baking paper. Turn the paper over and spread the plain chocolate over each marked circle, covering in a thin, even layer. Scatter flaked hazelnuts over four of the circles, then leave to set.

3 Melt the white chocolate in a heatproof bowl over hot water, then stir in the fromage frais and dry sherry. Fold in the chopped, toasted hazelnuts. Leave to cool until the mixture holds its shape.

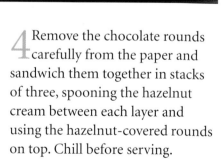

4 Remove the chocolate rounds carefully from the paper and sandwich them together in stacks of three, spooning the hazelnut cream between each layer and using the hazelnut-covered rounds on top. Chill before serving.

5 To serve, place the galettes on individual plates and decorate with chocolate-dipped physalis.

COOK'S TIP

The chocolate could be spread over heart shapes instead, for a special Valentine's Day dessert.

Chocolate and Chestnut Pots

Prepared in advance, these are the perfect ending for a dinner party. Remove them from the fridge about 30 minutes before serving, to allow them to "ripen".

Serves 6

250g/9oz plain chocolate

60ml/4 tbsp Madeira

25g/1oz/2 tbsp butter, diced

2 eggs, separated

225g/8oz/scant 1 cup unsweetened
   chestnut purée

crème fraîche or whipped double cream,
   to decorate

1 Make a few chocolate curls for decoration, then break the rest of the chocolate into squares and melt it with the Madeira in a saucepan over a gentle heat. Remove from the heat and add the butter, a few pieces at a time, stirring until melted and smooth.

COOK'S TIP

If Madeira is not available, use brandy or rum instead. These chocolate pots can be frozen successfully for up to 2 months.

2 Beat the egg yolks quickly into the mixture, then beat in the chestnut purée, mixing until smooth.

3 Whisk the egg whites in a clean, grease-free bowl until stiff. Stir about 15ml/1 tbsp of the whites into the chestnut mixture to lighten it, then fold in the rest smoothly and evenly.

4 Spoon the mixture into six small ramekin dishes and chill until set. Serve the pots topped with a generous spoonful of crème fraîche or whipped double cream and decorated with the plain chocolate curls.

Coffee Ice Cream with Caramelized Pecans

Coffee and sweetened nuts make a mouth-watering combination.

INGREDIENTS

Serves 4–6

For the ice cream

300ml/10fl oz/1¼ cups milk

1 tbsp demerara sugar

25g/1oz/6 tbsp finely ground coffee or 1 tbsp instant coffee granules

1 egg plus 2 yolks

300ml/10fl oz/1¼ cups double cream

1 tbsp caster sugar

For the pecans

115g/4oz/1 cup pecan halves

50g/2oz/4 tbsp soft dark brown sugar

1 Heat the milk and demerara sugar to boiling point. Remove from the heat and sprinkle on the coffee. Leave to stand for 2 minutes, then stir, cover and cool.

2 In a heatproof bowl, beat the egg and extra yolks until the mixture is thick and pale.

COOK'S TIP

You can give good-quality bought ice cream a fillip with the same nutty garnish.

3 Strain the coffee mixture into a clean pan, heat to boiling point, then pour on to the eggs in a steady stream, beating hard all the time.

4 Set the bowl over a pan of gently simmering water and stir until it thickens. Cool, then chill in the fridge.

5 Whip the cream with the caster sugar. Fold it into the coffee custard and freeze in a covered container. Beat twice at hourly intervals, then leave to freeze firm.

6 To caramelize the nuts, preheat the oven to 180°C/350°F/Gas 4. Spread the nuts on a baking sheet in a single layer. Put them into the oven for 10–15 minutes to toast until they release their fragrance.

7 On the top of the stove, dissolve the brown sugar in 2 tbsp water in a heavy-based pan, shaking it about over a low heat until the sugar dissolves completely and the syrup clears.

8 When the syrup begins to bubble, tip in the toasted pecans and cook for a minute or two over a medium heat until the syrup coats and clings to the nuts.

9 Spread the nuts on a lightly oiled baking sheet, separating them with the tip of a knife, and leave to cool. Store when cold in an airtight tin if they are not to be eaten on the same day.

10 Transfer the ice cream from the freezer to the fridge 30 minutes before scooping it into portions and serving with caramelized pecans.

White Chocolate Parfait

Everything you could wish for in a dessert; white and dark chocolate in one mouth-watering slice.

INGREDIENTS

Serves 10

225g/8oz white chocolate, chopped
600ml/1 pint/2½ cups whipping cream
120ml/4fl oz/½ cup milk
10 egg yolks
15ml/1 tbsp caster sugar
25g/1oz/scant ½ cup desiccated coconut
120ml/4fl oz/½ cup canned sweetened coconut milk
150g/5oz/1¼ cups unsalted macadamia nuts

For the chocolate icing
225g/8oz plain chocolate
75g/3oz/6 tbsp butter
20ml/generous 1 tbsp golden syrup
175ml/6fl oz/¾ cup whipping cream
curls of fresh coconut, to decorate

1 Line the base and sides of a 1.4 litre/2⅓ pint/6 cup terrine mould (25 x 10cm/10 x 4in) with clear film.

2 Place the chopped white chocolate and 50ml/2fl oz/¼ cup of the cream in the top of a double boiler or in a heatproof bowl set over hot water. Stir until melted and smooth. Set aside.

3 Put 250ml/8fl oz/1 cup of the cream and the milk in a pan and bring to boiling point.

4 Meanwhile, whisk the egg yolks and caster sugar together in a large bowl, until thick and pale.

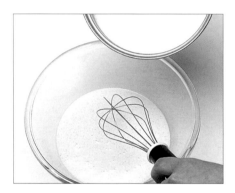

5 Add the hot cream mixture to the yolks, beating constantly. Pour back into the saucepan and cook over a low heat for 2–3 minutes, until thickened. Stir constantly and do not boil. Remove the pan from the heat.

6 Add the melted chocolate, desiccated coconut and coconut milk, then stir well and leave to cool.

7 Whip the remaining cream until thick, then fold into the chocolate and coconut mixture.

8 Put 475ml/16fl oz/2 cups of the parfait mixture in the prepared mould and spread evenly. Cover and freeze for about 2 hours, until just firm. Cover the remaining mixture and chill.

9 Scatter the macadamia nuts evenly over the frozen parfait. Pour in the remaining parfait mixture. Cover the terrine and freeze for 6–8 hours or overnight, until the parfait is firm.

10 To make the icing, melt the chocolate with the butter and syrup in the top of a double boiler set over hot water. Stir occasionally.

11 Heat the cream in a saucepan, until just simmering, then stir into the chocolate mixture. Remove the pan from the heat and leave to cool until lukewarm.

12 To turn out the parfait, wrap the terrine in a hot towel and set it upside down on a plate. Lift off the terrine mould, then peel off the clear film. Place the parfait on a rack over a baking sheet and pour the chocolate icing evenly over the top. Working quickly, smooth the icing down the sides with a palette knife. Leave to set slightly, then freeze for a further 3–4 hours. Cut into slices using a knife dipped in hot water. Serve, decorated with curls of fresh coconut.

White Chocolate Mousse with Dark Sauce

Creamy vanilla-flavoured white chocolate mousse is served with a dark rum and chocolate sauce.

INGREDIENTS

Serves 6–8

200g/7oz white chocolate, broken into
    squares
2 eggs, separated
60ml/4 tbsp caster sugar
300ml/½ pint/1¼ cups double cream
1 sachet powdered gelatine or alternative
150ml/¼ pint/⅔ cup Greek-style yogurt
10ml/2 tsp vanilla essence

For the sauce
50g/2oz plain chocolate, broken into
    squares
30ml/2 tbsp dark rum
60ml/4 tbsp single cream

1 Line a 1 litre/1¾ pint/4 cup loaf tin with non-stick baking paper or clear film. Melt the chocolate in a heatproof bowl over hot water, then remove from the heat.

2 Whisk the egg yolks and sugar in a bowl until pale and thick, then beat in the melted chocolate.

3 Heat the cream in a small saucepan until almost boiling, then remove from the heat. Sprinkle the powdered gelatine over, stirring gently until it is completely dissolved.

4 Then pour on to the chocolate mixture, whisking vigorously to mix until smooth.

5 Whisk the yogurt and vanilla essence into the mixture. In a clean, grease-free bowl, whisk the egg whites until stiff, then fold them into the mixture. Tip into the prepared loaf tin, level the surface and chill until set.

6 Make the sauce. Melt the chocolate with the rum and cream in a heatproof bowl over barely simmering water, stirring occasionally, then leave to cool.

7 When the mousse is set, remove it from the tin with the aid of the paper or clear film. Serve in thick slices with the cooled chocolate sauce poured round.

COOK'S TIP

Make sure the gelatine is completely dissolved in the cream before adding to the other ingredients.

Frozen Strawberry Mousse Cake

Children love this pretty dessert – it tastes just like an ice cream.

INGREDIENTS

Serves 4–6

425g/15oz can strawberries in syrup

15ml/1 tbsp/1 sachet powdered gelatine

6 trifle sponge cakes

45ml/3 tbsp strawberry jam

200ml/7fl oz/⅞ cup crème fraîche

200ml/7fl oz/⅞ cup whipped cream, to decorate

1 Strain the syrup from the strawberries into a large heatproof bowl. Sprinkle over the gelatine and stir well. Stand the bowl in a pan of hot water and stir until the gelatine has dissolved.

2 Leave to cool, then chill for just under 1 hour, until beginning to set. Meanwhile, cut the sponge cakes in half lengthways and spread the cut surfaces with the strawberry jam.

3 Carefully whisk the crème fraîche into the strawberry jelly, then whisk in the canned strawberries. Line a deep, 20cm/8in loose-based cake tin with non-stick baking paper.

4 Pour half the strawberry mousse mixture into the tin, arrange the sponge cakes over the surface, and then spoon over the remaining mousse mixture, pushing down any sponge cakes which rise up.

5 Freeze for 1–2 hours until firm. Remove the cake from the tin and carefully peel away the lining paper. Transfer to a serving plate. Decorate the mousse with whirls of whipped cream and a few strawberry leaves and a fresh strawberry, if you have them.

Iced Praline Torte

Make this elaborate torte several days ahead, decorate it and return it to the freezer until you are nearly ready to serve it. Allow the torte to stand at room temperature for an hour before serving, or leave it in the refrigerator overnight to soften.

Serves 8

115g/4oz/1 cup almonds or hazelnuts
115g/4oz/8 tbsp caster sugar
115g/4oz/⅔ cup raisins
90ml/6 tbsp rum or brandy
115g/4oz dark chocolate, broken into
   squares
30ml/2 tbsp milk
450ml/¾ pint/1⅞ cups double cream
30ml/2 tbsp strong black coffee
16 sponge finger biscuits

To finish
150ml/¼ pint/⅔ cup double cream
50g/2oz/½ cup flaked almonds, toasted
15g/½oz dark chocolate, melted

1 To make the praline, have ready an oiled cake tin or baking sheet. Put the nuts into a heavy-based pan with the sugar and heat gently until the sugar melts. Swirl the pan to coat the nuts in the hot sugar. Cook slowly until the nuts brown and the sugar caramelizes. Transfer the nuts quickly to the tin or baking sheet and leave them to cool completely. Break them up and grind them to a fine powder in a blender or food processor.

2 Soak the raisins in 45ml/3 tbsp of the rum or brandy for an hour (or better still overnight), so they soften and absorb the rum. Melt the chocolate with the milk in a bowl over a pan of hot, but not boiling water. Remove and allow to cool. Lightly grease a 1.2 litre/ 2 pint/5 cup loaf tin and line it with greaseproof paper.

3 Whisk the cream in a bowl until it holds soft peaks. Whisk in the cold chocolate. Then fold in the praline and the soaked raisins, with any liquid.

4 Mix the coffee and remaining rum or brandy in a shallow dish. Dip in the sponge fingers and arrange half in a layer over the base of the prepared loaf tin.

5 Cover with the chocolate mixture and add another layer of soaked sponge fingers. Leave in the freezer overnight.

6 Whip the double cream for the topping. Dip the tin briefly into warm water to loosen it and turn the torte out on to a serving plate. Cover with the whipped cream, sprinkle the top with toasted flaked almonds and drizzle the melted chocolate over the top. Return the torte to the freezer until it is needed.

COOK'S TIP

Make the praline in advance and store it in an airtight jar until needed.

Blackcurrant Sorbet

Blackcurrants make a vibrant and intensely flavoured sorbet.

INGREDIENTS

Serves 4–6

90g/3½oz/½ cup caster sugar

500g/1¼lb blackcurrants

juice of ½ lemon

15ml/1 tbsp egg white

mint leaves, to decorate

1 In a small saucepan over a medium-high heat, bring the sugar and 120ml/4fl oz/½ cup water to the boil, stirring until the sugar dissolves. Boil the syrup for 2 minutes, then remove the pan from the heat and set aside to cool.

2 Remove the blackcurrants from the stalks by pulling them through the tines of a fork.

3 In a blender or food processor fitted with a metal blade, process the blackcurrants and lemon juice until smooth. Alternatively, chop the black-currants coarsely, then add the lemon juice. Mix in the sugar syrup.

4 Press the purée through a sieve to remove the seeds.

5 Pour the blackcurrant purée into a non-metallic, freezer-proof dish. Cover the dish with clear film or a lid and freeze until the sorbet is nearly firm, but still a bit slushy.

6 Cut the sorbet into pieces and put into the blender or food processor. Process until smooth, then with the machine running, add the egg white and process until well mixed. Tip the sorbet back into the dish and freeze until almost firm. Chop the sorbet again and process until smooth.

7 Serve immediately or freeze, tightly covered, for up to 1 week. Allow to soften for 5–10 minutes at room temperature before serving, decorated with mint leaves.

Chocolate Ice Cream

Use good quality plain or cooking chocolate for the best flavour.

INGREDIENTS

Makes about 900ml/1½ pints/3¾ cups

750ml/1¼ pints/3 cups milk

10cm/4in piece vanilla pod

4 egg yolks

150g/5oz/¾ cup granulated sugar

225g/8oz cooking chocolate, melted

1 To make the custard, heat the milk with the vanilla pod in a small saucepan. Remove from the heat as soon as small bubbles start to form. Do not boil.

2 Beat the egg yolks with a wire whisk or electric beater. Gradually incorporate the sugar, and continue beating for about 5 minutes until the mixture is pale yellow. Strain the milk. Slowly add it to the egg mixture drop by drop.

3 Pour the mixture into a double boiler with the melted chocolate. Stir over moderate heat until the water in the pan is boiling, and the custard thickens enough to lightly coat the back of a spoon. Remove from the heat and allow to cool.

4 Freeze in an ice-cream maker, or if you do not have an ice-cream maker, pour the mixture into a metal or plastic freezer container and freeze until set, about 3 hours. Remove from the container and chop roughly into 7.5cm/3in pieces. Place in the bowl of a food processor and process until smooth. Return to the freezer container, and freeze again until firm. Repeat the freezing-chopping process 2 or 3 times, until a smooth consistency is reached.

Frozen Grand Marnier Soufflés

These sophisticated little puddings are always appreciated and make a wonderful end to a meal.

INGREDIENTS

Serves 8

200g/7oz/1 cup caster sugar

6 large eggs, separated

250ml/8fl oz/1 cup milk

15g/½oz powdered gelatine, soaked in 45ml/3 tbsp cold water

450ml/¾ pint/1⅞ cups double cream

60ml/4 tbsp Grand Marnier

1 Tie a double collar of grease-proof paper round eight ramekin dishes. Put 75g/3oz/6 tbsp of the sugar in a bowl with the egg yolks and whisk until pale.

2 Heat the milk until almost boiling and pour it on to the yolks, whisking all the time. Return to the pan and stir it over a gentle heat until it is thick enough to coat a spoon. Remove the pan from the heat and stir in the soaked gelatine. Pour into a bowl and leave to cool. Whisk occasionally, until it is on the point of setting.

3 Put the remaining sugar in a pan with 45ml/3 tbsp water and dissolve it over a low heat. Bring to the boil and boil rapidly until it reaches the soft ball stage or 119°C/246°F on a sugar thermometer. Remove from the heat. In a clean bowl, whisk the egg whites until they are stiff. Pour the hot syrup on to the whites, whisking all the time. Set aside and leave to cool.

4 Whisk the cream until it holds soft peaks. Add the Grand Marnier to the cold custard and fold the custard into the cold meringue, with the cream. Quickly pour into the prepared ramekin dishes. Freeze overnight. Remove the paper collars. Leave the soufflés at room temperature for 30 minutes before serving.

Double Chocolate Snowball

This is an ideal party dessert as it can be prepared at least one day ahead and decorated on the day.

INGREDIENTS

Serves 12–14

350g/12oz plain chocolate, chopped

285g/10½oz/1½ cups caster sugar

275g/10oz/1¼ cups unsalted butter, cut into small pieces

8 eggs

50ml/2fl oz/¼ cup orange-flavoured liqueur or brandy (optional)

cocoa (optional), for dusting

For the white chocolate cream

200g/7oz fine quality white chocolate, broken into pieces

475ml/16fl oz/2 cups double or whipping cream

30ml/2 tbsp orange flavour liqueur (optional)

1 Preheat the oven to 180°C/ 350°F/Gas 4. Line a 1.75 litre/ 3 pint/7½ cup round ovenproof bowl with aluminium foil, smoothing the sides. In a bowl over a pan of simmering water, melt the plain chocolate. Add the sugar and stir until it dissolves. Strain into a medium bowl. With an electric mixer at low speed, beat in the butter, then the eggs, one at a time, beating well after each addition. Stir in the liqueur or brandy, if using, and pour into the prepared bowl. Tap gently to release any large air bubbles.

2 Bake for 1¼–1½ hours until the surface is firm and slightly risen, but cracked. The centre will still be wobbly: this will set on cooling. Remove to a rack to cool to room temperature. Cover with a plate, then cover completely with clear film or foil and chill overnight. To unmould, remove plate and film or foil and invert the mould on to a plate; shake firmly to release. Peel off the foil. Cover until ready to decorate.

3 Process the white chocolate in a blender or food processor until fine crumbs form. In a small saucepan, heat 120ml/4fl oz/½ cup of the cream until just beginning to simmer. With the food processor running, pour the cream through the feed tube and process until the chocolate is completely melted. Strain into a medium bowl and cool to room temperature, stirring occasionally.

4 Beat the remaining cream until soft peaks form, add the liqueur, if using, and beat for 30 seconds or until the cream just holds its shape. Fold a spoonful of cream into the chocolate then fold in the remaining cream. Spoon into an icing bag fitted with a star tip and pipe rosettes over the surface. If liked, dust with cocoa.

HOT
PUDDINGS

Hot Chocolate Zabaglione

A deliciously chocolate-flavoured variation of a classic Italian dessert.

Serves 6

6 egg yolks

150g/5oz/¾ cup caster sugar

45ml/3 tbsp cocoa powder

200ml/7fl oz/⅞ cup Marsala

cocoa powder or icing sugar, for dusting

almond biscuits, to serve

1 Half fill a medium saucepan with water and bring to simmering point.

2 Place the egg yolks and sugar in a heatproof bowl and whisk until the mixture is pale and all the sugar has dissolved.

3 Add the cocoa and Marsala, then place the bowl over the simmering water. Whisk until the consistency of the mixture is smooth, thick and foamy.

4 Pour quickly into tall heatproof glasses, dust lightly with cocoa or icing sugar and serve immediately with almond biscuits.

Chocolate and Orange Scotch Pancakes

Fabulous baby pancakes in a rich creamy orange liqueur sauce.

INGREDIENTS

Serves 4

115g/4oz/1 cup self-raising flour

30ml/2 tbsp cocoa powder

2 eggs

50g/2oz plain chocolate, broken into squares

200ml/7fl oz/⅞ cup milk

finely grated rind of 1 orange

30ml/2 tbsp orange juice

butter or oil, for frying

60ml/4 tbsp chocolate curls, for sprinkling

For the sauce

2 large oranges

30ml/2 tbsp unsalted butter

45ml/3 tbsp light muscovado sugar

250ml/8fl oz/1 cup crème fraîche

30ml/2 tbsp Grand Marnier or Cointreau

1 Sift the flour and cocoa into a bowl and make a well in the centre. Add the eggs and beat well, gradually incorporating the surrounding dry ingredients to make a smooth batter.

2 Mix the chocolate and milk in a saucepan. Heat gently until the chocolate has melted, then beat into the batter until smooth and bubbly. Stir in the grated orange rind and juice.

3 Heat a large heavy-based frying pan or griddle. Grease with a little butter or oil. Drop large spoonfuls of batter on to the hot surface. Cook over a moderate heat. When the pancakes are lightly browned underneath and bubbly on top, flip them over to cook the other side. Slide on to a plate and keep hot, then make more in the same way.

4 Make the sauce. Grate the rind of 1 of the oranges into a bowl and set aside. Peel both oranges, taking care to remove all the pith, then slice the flesh fairly thinly.

5 Heat the butter and sugar in a wide, shallow pan over a low heat, stirring until the sugar dissolves. Stir in the crème fraîche and heat gently.

6 Add the pancakes and orange slices to the sauce, heat gently for 1–2 minutes, then spoon over the liqueur. Sprinkle with the reserved orange rind. Scatter over the chocolate curls and serve the pancakes at once.

Amaretto Soufflé

A mouth-watering soufflé with more than a hint of Amaretto liqueur.

INGREDIENTS

Serves 6

130g/4½oz/½ cup caster sugar
6 amaretti biscuits, coarsely crushed
90ml/6 tbsp Amaretto liqueur
4 eggs, separated, plus 1 egg white
30ml/2 tbsp plain flour
250ml/8fl oz/1 cup milk
pinch of cream of tartar (if needed)
icing sugar, for dusting

1 Preheat the oven to 200°C/ 400°F/Gas 6. Butter a 1.5 litre/ 2½ pint/6¼ cup soufflé dish and sprinkle it with a little of the caster sugar.

2 Put the biscuits in a bowl. Sprinkle them with 30ml/ 2 tbsp of the Amaretto liqueur and set aside.

3 In another bowl, carefully mix the 4 egg yolks, 30ml/ 2 tbsp of the sugar and all the flour.

4 Heat the milk just to the boil in a heavy saucepan. Gradually add the hot milk to the egg mixture, stirring.

5 Pour the mixture back into the pan. Set over a low heat and simmer gently for 3–4 minutes or until thickened, stirring occasionally.

6 Add the remaining Amaretto liqueur. Remove from the heat.

7 In a scrupulously clean, grease-free bowl, whisk the 5 egg whites until they hold soft peaks. (If not using a copper bowl, add the cream of tartar as soon as the whites are frothy.) Add the remaining sugar and continue whisking until stiff.

8 Add about one-quarter of the whites to the liqueur mixture and stir in with a rubber spatula. Add the remaining whites and fold in gently.

9 Spoon half of the mixture into the prepared soufflé dish. Cover with a layer of the moistened amaretti biscuits, then spoon the remaining soufflé mixture on top.

10 Bake for 20 minutes or until the soufflé is risen and lightly browned. Sprinkle with sifted icing sugar and serve immediately.

Hot Mocha Rum Soufflés

Serve these superb soufflés as soon as they are cooked for a fantastic finale to a dinner party.

INGREDIENTS

Serves 6

25g/1oz/2 tbsp unsalted butter, melted

65g/2½ oz/generous ½ cup cocoa powder

75g/3oz/generous ⅓ cup caster sugar

60ml/4 tbsp strong black coffee

30ml/2 tbsp dark rum

6 egg whites

icing sugar, for dusting

1 Preheat the oven with a baking sheet inside to 190°C/375°F/ Gas 5. Grease six 250ml/8fl oz/ 1 cup soufflé dishes with the melted butter.

2 Mix 15ml/1 tbsp of the cocoa with 15ml/1 tbsp of the caster sugar in a bowl. Tip the mixture into each of the dishes in turn, rotating them so that they are evenly coated.

3 Mix the remaining cocoa with the coffee and rum.

4 Whisk the egg whites in a clean, grease-free bowl until they form firm peaks. Whisk in the remaining caster sugar. Stir a generous spoonful of the whites into the cocoa mixture to lighten it, then gently fold in the remaining whites.

5 Spoon the mixture into the prepared dishes, smoothing the tops. Place on the hot baking sheet, and bake for 12–15 minutes or until well risen. Serve the soufflés immediately, lightly dusted with icing sugar.

COOK'S TIP

When serving the soufflés at the end of a dinner party, prepare them just before the meal is served. Pop in the oven as soon as the main course is finished and serve freshly baked.

Gingerbread Upside-down Pudding

A proper pudding goes down well on a cold winter's day. This one is quite quick and easy to make and looks very impressive.

Serves 4–6

sunflower oil, for brushing

15ml/1 tbsp soft brown sugar

4 medium peaches, halved and stoned, or canned peach halves

8 walnut halves

For the base

130g/4½ oz/generous 1 cup wholemeal flour

2.5ml/½ tsp bicarbonate of soda

7.5ml/1½ tsp ground ginger

5ml/1 tsp ground cinnamon

115g/4oz/½ cup molasses sugar

1 egg

120ml/4fl oz/½ cup skimmed milk

50ml/2fl oz/¼ cup sunflower oil

1 Preheat the oven to 180°C/ 350°F/Gas 4. For the topping, brush the base and sides of a 23cm/9in round springform cake tin with oil. Sprinkle the sugar over the base.

2 Arrange the peaches cut-side down in the tin with a walnut half in each.

3 Sift together the flour, bicarbonate of soda, ginger and cinnamon, then stir in the sugar. Beat together the egg, milk and oil, then mix into the dry ingredients.

4 Pour the mixture evenly over the peaches and bake for 35–40 minutes, until firm to the touch. Turn out and serve hot.

Peach Cobbler

A satisfying pudding which combines fresh peaches with almond-flavoured pastry.

Serves 6

about 1.5kg/3lb peaches, peeled and sliced

45ml/3 tbsp caster sugar

30ml/2 tbsp peach brandy

15ml/1 tbsp fresh lemon juice

15ml/1 tbsp cornflour

For the topping

115g/4oz/1 cup plain flour

7.5ml/1½ tsp baking powder

1.5ml/¼ tsp salt

40g/1½oz/¼ cup finely ground almonds

50g/2oz/¼ cup caster sugar

50g/2oz/4 tbsp butter or margarine

85ml/3fl oz/⅜ cup milk

1.5ml/¼ tsp almond essence

1 Preheat the oven to 220°C/425°F/Gas 7. In a bowl, toss the peaches with the sugar, peach brandy, lemon juice and cornflour, then spoon the peach mixture into a 2 litre/3½ pint/8 cup baking dish.

2 For the topping, sift the flour, baking powder and salt into a mixing bowl. Stir in the ground almonds and all but 1 tablespoon of the sugar. With two knives, or a pastry blender, cut in the butter or margarine until the mixture resembles coarse breadcrumbs.

3 Add the milk and almond essence and stir until the topping mixture is just combined.

4 Drop the topping in spoonfuls on to the peaches. Sprinkle the top with the remaining tablespoon of sugar.

5 Bake until the cobbler topping is browned, 30–35 minutes. Serve hot with ice cream or crème fraîche, if preferred.

Baked Apples with Caramel Sauce

The creamy caramel sauce turns this simple country dessert into a more sophisticated delicacy.

INGREDIENTS

Serves 6

3 Granny Smith apples, cored but not
  peeled
3 Red Delicious apples, cored but not
  peeled
150g/5oz/¾ cup light brown sugar
2.5ml/½ tsp grated nutmeg
1.5ml/¼ tsp freshly ground black pepper
40g/1½ oz/¼ cup walnut pieces
40g/1½ oz/scant ¼ cup sultanas
50g/2oz/4 tbsp butter or margarine, diced

For the caramel sauce
15g/½oz/1 tbsp butter or margarine
120ml/4fl oz/½ cup whipping cream

1 Preheat the oven to 190°C/ 375°F/Gas 5. Grease a baking tin just large enough to hold the apples.

2 With a small knife, cut at an angle to enlarge the core opening at the stem-end of each apple to about 2.5cm/1in in diameter. (The opening should resemble a funnel in shape.)

3 Arrange the apples in the prepared tin, stem-end up.

4 In a small saucepan, combine 175ml/6fl oz/¾ cup of water with the brown sugar, nutmeg and pepper. Bring the mixture to the boil, stirring. Boil for 6 minutes.

5 Mix together the walnuts and sultanas. Spoon some of the walnut-sultana mixture into the opening in each apple.

6 Top each apple with some of the diced butter or margarine.

7 Spoon the brown sugar sauce over and around the apples. Bake, basting occasionally with the sauce, until the apples are just tender, 45–50 minutes. Transfer the apples to a serving dish, reserving the brown sugar sauce in the baking tin. Keep the apples warm.

8 For the caramel sauce, mix the butter or margarine, cream and reserved brown sugar sauce in a saucepan. Bring to the boil, stirring occasionally, and simmer until thickened, about 2 minutes. Leave the sauce to cool slightly before serving.

VARIATION

Use a mixture of firm red and gold pears instead of the apples, preparing them in the same way. Cook for 10 minutes longer.

Baked Apples with Apricot Filling

An alternative stuffing mixture for baked apples, with a refreshing fruit flavour.

INGREDIENTS

Serves 6

75g/3oz/scant ½ cup chopped, ready-to-eat dried apricots

50g/2oz/½ cup chopped walnuts

5ml/1 tsp grated lemon rind

2.5ml/½ tsp ground cinnamon

90g/3½oz/½ cup soft light brown sugar

25g/1oz/2 tbsp butter, at room temperature

6 large eating apples

15ml/1 tbsp melted butter

1 Preheat the oven to 190°C/375°F/Gas 5. Place the apricots, walnuts, lemon rind and cinnamon in a bowl. Add the sugar and butter and stir until thoroughly mixed.

2 Core the apples, without cutting all the way through to the base. Peel the top of each apple and then slightly widen the top of each opening to make room for the filling.

3 Spoon the filling into the apples, packing it down lightly.

4 Place the stuffed apples in an ovenproof dish large enough to hold them all comfortably side by side.

5 Brush the apples with the melted butter. Bake for 45–50 minutes, until they are tender. Serve hot.

COOK'S TIP

Accompany with real custard, Crème Anglaise, made using cream, egg yolks, caster sugar and a few drops of vanilla essence.

Pears in Chocolate Fudge Blankets

Warm poached pears coated in a
rich chocolate fudge sauce – who
could resist?

INGREDIENTS

Serves 6

6 ripe eating pears

30ml/2 tbsp lemon juice

75g/3oz/scant ½ cup caster sugar

1 cinnamon stick

For the sauce

200ml/7fl oz/⅞ cup double cream

150g/5oz/scant 1 cup light muscovado
  sugar

25g/1oz/2 tbsp unsalted butter

60ml/4 tbsp golden syrup

120ml/4fl oz/½ cup milk

200g/7oz plain dark chocolate, broken
  into squares

1 Peel the pears thinly, leaving
the stalks on. Scoop out the
cores from the base. Brush the cut
surfaces with lemon juice to
prevent browning.

2 Place the sugar and 300ml/
½ pint/1¼ cups of water in a
large saucepan. Heat gently until
the sugar dissolves. Add the pears
and cinnamon stick with any
remaining lemon juice, and, if
necessary, a little more water, so
that the pears are almost covered.

3 Bring to the boil, then lower the
heat, cover the pan and simmer
the pears gently for 15-20 minutes.

4 Meanwhile, make the sauce.
Place the cream, sugar, butter,
golden syrup and milk in a heavy-
based saucepan. Heat gently until
the sugar has dissolved and the
butter and syrup have melted, then
bring to the boil. Boil, stirring
constantly, for about 5 minutes or
until thick and smooth.

5 Remove the pan from the heat
and stir in the chocolate, a
little at a time, until melted.

6 Using a slotted spoon, transfer
the poached pears to a dish.
Keep hot. Boil the syrup rapidly to
reduce to about 45–60ml/3–4 tbsp.
Remove the cinnamon stick and
gently stir the syrup into the
chocolate sauce.

7 Serve the pears in individual
bowls or on dessert plates, with
the hot chocolate fudge sauce
spooned over.

Sticky Toffee Pudding

Filling, warming and packed with calories, but still everyone's favourite pudding.

Serves 6

115g/4oz/1 cup toasted walnuts, chopped

175g/6oz/¾ cup butter

175g/6oz/scant 1 cup soft brown sugar

60ml/4 tbsp single cream

30ml/2 tbsp lemon juice

2 eggs, beaten

115g/4oz/1 cup self-raising flour

1 Grease a 900ml/1½ pint/ 3¾ cup pudding basin and add half the walnuts.

2 Heat 50g/2oz/4 tbsp of the butter with 50g/2oz/4 tbsp of the sugar, the cream and 15ml/ 1 tbsp lemon juice in a small pan, stirring until smooth. Pour half into the pudding basin, then swirl to coat it a little way up the sides.

3 Beat the remaining butter and sugar until light and fluffy, then gradually beat in the eggs. Fold in the flour and the remaining nuts and lemon juice and spoon into the bowl.

4 Cover the bowl with grease-proof paper with a pleat folded in the centre, then tie securely with string.

5 Steam the pudding for about 1¼ hours, until it is set in the centre.

6 Just before serving, gently warm the remaining sauce. Unmould the pudding on to a warm plate and pour over the warm sauce.

Chocolate and Orange Soufflé

The base in this soufflé is an easy-to-make semolina mixture, rather than the thick white sauce that most soufflés call for.

Serves 4

600ml/1 pint/2½ cups milk

50g/2oz/generous ⅓ cup semolina

50g/2oz/scant ¼ cup brown sugar

grated rind of 1 orange

90ml/6 tbsp fresh orange juice

3 eggs, separated

65g/2½oz plain chocolate, grated

icing sugar, for sprinkling

1 Preheat the oven to 200°C/400°F/Gas 6. Butter a shallow 1.75 litre/3 pint/7½ cup ovenproof dish.

2 Pour the milk into a heavy-based saucepan, sprinkle over the semolina and brown sugar, then heat, stirring the mixture all the time, until boiling and thickened.

3 Remove the pan from the heat, beat in the orange rind and juice, egg yolks and all but 15ml/ 1 tbsp of the grated chocolate.

4 Whisk the egg whites until stiff, then lightly fold into the semolina mixture in three batches. Spoon into the buttered dish and bake for about 30 minutes, until just set in the centre. Sprinkle with the reserved chocolate and the icing sugar.

Queen of Puddings

This hot pudding was developed from a seventeenth-century recipe by Queen Victoria's chefs and named in her honour.

INGREDIENTS

Serves 4

75g/3oz/1½ cups fresh breadcrumbs

60ml/4 tbsp caster sugar, plus 5ml/1 tsp

grated rind of 1 lemon

600ml/1 pint/2½ cups milk

4 eggs

45ml/3 tbsp raspberry jam, warmed

1 Preheat the oven to 160°C/ 325°F/Gas 3. Stir the breadcrumbs, 30ml/2 tbsp of the sugar and the lemon rind together in a bowl. Bring the milk to the boil in a saucepan, then stir into the breadcrumb mixture.

2 Separate three of the eggs and beat the yolks with the whole egg. Stir into the breadcrumb mixture, pour into a buttered baking dish and leave to stand for 30 minutes, then bake the pudding for 50–60 minutes, until set.

COOK'S TIP
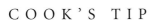

Ring the changes by using another flavoured jam, lemon curd, marmalade or fruit purée.

3 Whisk the three egg whites in a large, clean bowl until stiff but not dry, then gradually whisk in the remaining 30ml/2 tbsp caster sugar until the mixture is thick and glossy, taking care not to overwhip.

4 Spread the jam over the pudding, then spoon over the meringue to cover the top completely. Sprinkle the remaining sugar over the meringue, then bake for a further 15 minutes, until the meringue is beginning to turn a light golden colour.

Apple Couscous Pudding

*This unusual couscous mixture
makes a delicious family pudding
with a rich fruity flavour, but
virtually no fat.*

INGREDIENTS

Serves 4

600ml/1 pint/2½ cups apple juice

115g/4oz/⅔ cup couscous

40g/1½oz/scant ¼ cup sultanas

2.5ml/½ tsp mixed spice

1 large Bramley cooking apple, peeled,
   cored and sliced

25g/1oz/2 tbsp demerara sugar

natural low fat yogurt, to serve

1 Preheat the oven to
200°C/400°F/Gas 6. Place the
apple juice, couscous, sultanas and
spice in a pan and bring to the
boil, stirring. Cover and simmer
for 10–12 minutes, until all the free
liquid is absorbed.

COOK'S TIP
∽

To ring the changes, substitute
other dried fruits for the sultanas
in this recipe – try chopped dates
or ready-to-eat pears, figs or
apricots.

2 Spoon half the couscous
mixture into a 1.2 litre/2 pint/
5 cup ovenproof dish and top with
half the apple slices. Top with the
remaining couscous.

3 Arrange the remaining apple
slices overlapping over the top
and sprinkle with demerara sugar.
Bake for 25–30 minutes, or until
the apples are golden brown.
Serve hot with yogurt.

Chocolate Crêpes with Plums and Port

A good dinner party dessert, this dish can be made in advance and always looks impressive.

INGREDIENTS

Serves 6

50g/2oz plain chocolate, broken into squares

200ml/7fl oz/⁷⁄₈ cup milk

120ml/4fl oz/½ cup single cream

30ml/2 tbsp cocoa powder

115g/4oz/1 cup plain flour

2 eggs

For the filling

500g/1¼lb red or golden plums

50g/2oz/¼ cup caster sugar

30ml/2 tbsp port

oil, for frying

175g/6oz/¾ cup crème fraîche

For the sauce

150g/5oz plain chocolate, broken into squares

175ml/6fl oz/¾ cup double cream

30ml/2 tbsp port

1 Place the chocolate in a saucepan with the milk. Heat gently until the chocolate has dissolved. Pour into a blender or food processor and add the cream, cocoa powder, flour and eggs. Process until smooth, then tip into a jug and chill for 30 minutes.

2 Meanwhile, make the filling. Halve and stone the plums. Place them in a saucepan and add the sugar and 30ml/2 tbsp of water. Bring to the boil, then lower the heat, cover, and simmer for about 10 minutes or until the plums are tender. Stir in the port; simmer for a further 30 seconds. Remove the pan from the heat and keep warm.

3 Have ready a sheet of non-stick baking paper. Heat a crêpe pan, grease it lightly with a little oil, then pour in just enough batter to cover the base of the pan, swirling to coat it evenly.

4 Cook until the crêpe has set, then flip it over to cook the other side. Slide the crêpe out on to the sheet of paper, then cook 9–11 more crêpes in the same way.

5 Make the sauce. Combine the chocolate and cream in a saucepan. Heat gently, stirring until smooth. Add the port and heat gently, stirring, for 1 minute.

6 Divide the plum filling between the crêpes, add a dollop of crème fraîche to each and roll them up carefully. Serve in shallow plates, with the chocolate sauce spooned over the top.

Chocolate Soufflé Crêpes

A non-stick pan is ideal as it does not need greasing between each crêpe. Serve two crêpes per person.

INGREDIENTS

Makes 12 crêpes

75g/3oz/⅔ cup plain flour
15ml/1 tbsp unsweetened cocoa
5ml/1 tsp caster sugar
pinch of salt
5ml/1 tsp ground cinnamon
2 eggs
175ml/6fl oz/¾ cup milk
5ml/1 tsp vanilla essence
50g/2oz/4 tbsp unsalted butter, melted
icing sugar, for dusting
raspberries, pineapple and mint sprigs, to decorate

For the pineapple syrup

½ medium pineapple, peeled, cored and finely chopped
30ml/2 tbsp natural maple syrup
5ml/1 tsp cornflour
½ cinnamon stick
30ml/2 tbsp rum

For the soufflé filling

250g/9oz semi-sweet or bittersweet chocolate
85ml/3fl oz/⅓ cup double cream
3 eggs, separated
25g/1oz/2 tbsp caster sugar

1 Prepare the syrup. In a saucepan over medium heat, bring the pineapple, 125ml/4fl oz/½ cup water, maple syrup, cornflour and cinnamon stick to the boil. Simmer for 2–3 minutes until the sauce thickens, whisking frequently. Remove from the heat; discard the cinnamon. Pour into a bowl, stir in the rum and chill.

2 Prepare the crêpes. In a bowl, sift the flour, cocoa, sugar, salt and cinnamon. Stir to blend, then make a well in the centre. In a bowl, beat the eggs, milk and vanilla. Gradually add to the well, whisking in flour from the side to form a smooth batter. Stir in half the butter and pour the batter into a jug. Allow to stand for 1 hour.

3 Heat an 18–20cm/7–8in crêpe pan. Brush with butter. Stir the batter. Pour 45ml/3 tbsp batter into the pan; swirl the pan quickly to cover the bottom with a thin layer. Cook over medium-high heat for 1–2 minutes until the bottom is golden. Turn over and cook for 30–45 seconds, then turn on to a plate. Stack the crêpes between non-stick baking paper.

4 Prepare the filling. In a small saucepan, over medium heat, melt the chocolate and cream until smooth, stirring frequently.

5 In a bowl, beat the yolks with half the sugar for 3–5 minutes, until light and creamy. Gradually beat in the chocolate mixture. Allow to cool. In a large bowl, beat the egg whites until soft peaks form. Gradually beat in the remaining sugar until stiff. Beat in a spoonful of egg whites to the chocolate mixture, then fold in the remainder.

6 Preheat the oven to 200°C/ 400°F/Gas 6. Lay a crêpe on a plate. Spoon a little soufflé mixture on to the crêpe, spreading it to the edge. Fold the bottom half over the soufflé mixture, then fold in half again to form a filled "triangle". Place on a buttered baking sheet. Repeat with the remaining crêpes.

7 Brush the tops with melted butter and bake for 15–20 minutes until fluffy. Dust with icing sugar and garnish with raspberries, pineapple, mint and a spoonful of pineapple syrup.

Christmas Pudding

This recipe makes enough to fill one 1.2 litre/2 pint/5 cup basin or two 600ml/1 pint/2½ cup basins. It can be made up to a month before Christmas and stored in a cool, dry place. Steam the pudding for 2 hours before serving. Serve with brandy or rum butter, whisky sauce, custard or whipped cream, topped with a decorative sprig of holly.

INGREDIENTS

Serves 8

115g/4oz/½ cup butter
225g/8oz/1 heaped cup soft dark brown
    sugar
50g/2oz/½ cup self-raising flour
5ml/1tsp ground mixed spice
1.5ml/¼ tsp grated nutmeg
2.5ml/½ tsp ground cinnamon
2 eggs
115g/4oz/2 cups fresh white breadcrumbs
175g/6oz/generous 1 cup sultanas
175g/6oz/generous 1 cup raisins
115g/4oz/½ cup currants
25g/1oz/3 tbsp mixed candied peel,
    chopped finely
25g/1oz/¼ cup chopped almonds
1 small cooking apple, peeled, cored and
    coarsely grated
finely grated rind of 1 orange or lemon
juice of 1 orange or lemon, made up to
    150ml/¼ pint/⅔ cup with brandy, rum
    or sherry

1 Cut a disc of greaseproof paper to fit the base of the basin(s) and butter the disc and basin(s).

2 Whisk the butter and sugar together until soft. Beat in the flour, spices and eggs. Stir in the remaining ingredients thoroughly. The mixture should have a soft dropping consistency.

3 Turn the mixture into the greased basin(s) and level the top with a spoon.

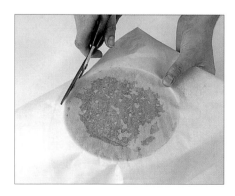

4 Cover with another disc of buttered greaseproof paper.

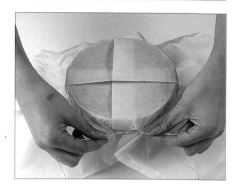

5 Make two pleats across the centre of a piece of greaseproof paper and cover the basin(s) with it, tying it in place with string under the rim. Cut off the excess paper. Pleat a piece of foil in the same way and cover the basin(s) with it, tucking it round the bowl neatly, under the greaseproof frill. Tie another piece of string round and across the top, as a handle.

6 Place the basin(s) in a steamer over a pan of simmering water and steam for 6 hours. Alternatively, put the basin(s) into a large pan and pour round enough boiling water to come halfway up the basin(s) and cover the pan with a tight-fitting lid. Check the water is simmering and top it up with boiling water as it evaporates. When the pudding(s) have cooked, leave to cool completely. Then remove the foil and greaseproof paper. Wipe the basin(s) clean and replace the greaseproof paper and foil with clean pieces, ready for reheating.

TO SERVE

Steam for 2 hours. Turn on to a plate and leave to stand for 5 minutes, before removing the pudding basin (the steam will rise to the top of the basin and help to loosen the pudding). Decorate with a sprig of holly.

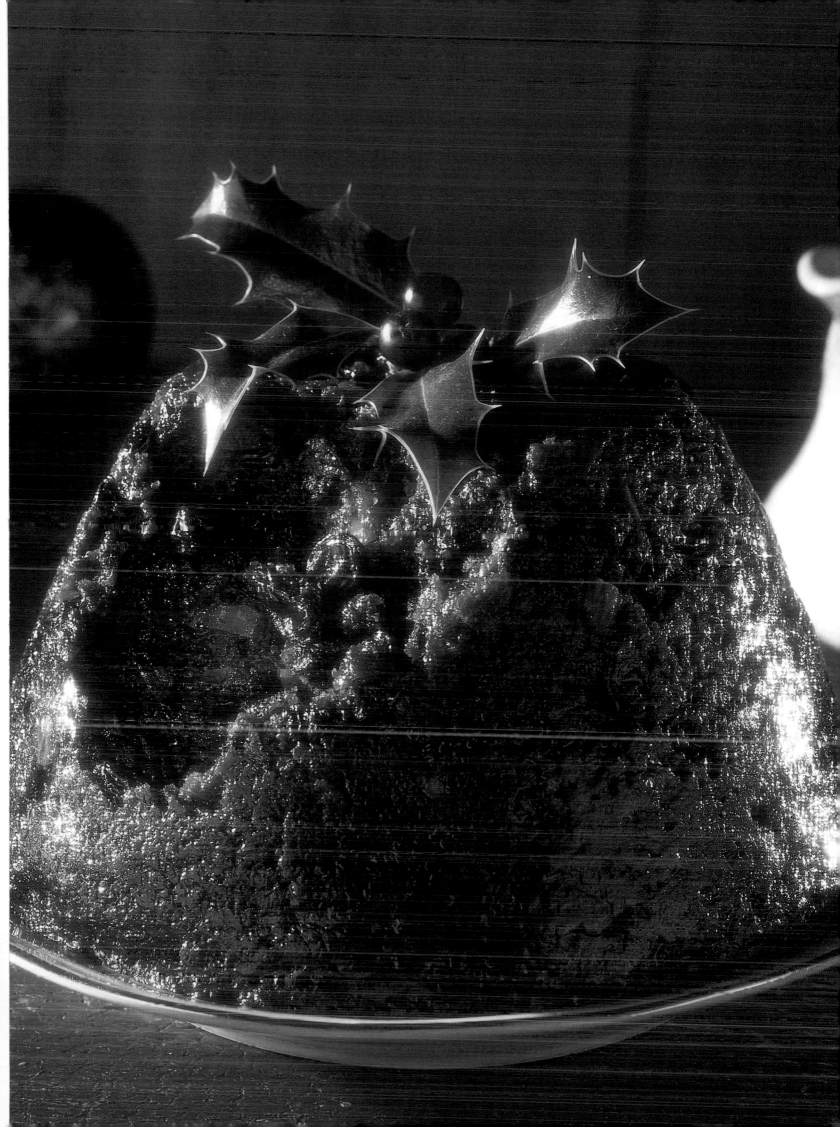

Chocolate Almond Meringue Pie

This dream dessert combines three very popular flavours: velvety chocolate filling on a light orange pastry case, topped with fluffy meringue.

INGREDIENTS

Serves 6

175g/6oz/1½ cups plain flour
50g/2oz/⅓ cup ground rice
150g/5oz/⅔ cup unsalted butter
finely grated rind of 1 orange
1 egg yolk
flaked almonds and melted plain dark
    chocolate, to decorate

For the filling

150g/5oz plain dark chocolate, broken
    into squares
50g/2oz/4 tbsp unsalted butter, softened
75g/3oz/⅓ cup caster sugar
10ml/2 tsp cornflour
4 egg yolks
75g/3oz/¾ cup ground almonds

For the meringue

3 egg whites
150g/5oz/¾ cup caster sugar

1 Sift the flour and ground rice into a bowl. Rub in the butter until the mixture resembles breadcrumbs. Stir in the orange rind. Add the egg yolk; bring the dough together. Roll out and use to line a 23cm/9in round flan tin. Chill for 30 minutes.

2 Preheat the oven to 190°C/ 375°F/Gas 5. Prick the pastry base all over with a fork, cover with greaseproof paper weighed down with baking beans and bake blind for 10 minutes. Remove the pastry case; take out the baking beans and paper.

3 Make the filling. Melt the chocolate in a heatproof bowl over hot water. Cream the butter with the sugar in a bowl, then beat in the cornflour and egg yolks. Fold in the almonds, then the chocolate. Spread in the pastry case. Bake for a further 10 minutes.

4 Make the meringue. Whisk the egg whites until stiff, then gradually add half the caster sugar. Fold in remaining sugar.

5 Spoon the meringue over the chocolate filling, lifting if up with the back of the spoon to form peaks. Reduce the oven temperature to 180°C/350°F/Gas 4 and bake the pie for 15–20 minutes or until the topping is pale gold. Serve warm, scattered with almonds and drizzled with melted chocolate.

Chocolate Chip and Banana Pudding

Hot and steamy, this superb light pudding tastes extra special served with chocolate sauce.

INGREDIENTS

Serves 4

200g/7oz/1¾ cups self-raising flour
75g/3oz/6 tbsp unsalted butter or
    margarine
2 ripe bananas
75g/3oz/⅓ cup caster sugar
60ml/4 tbsp milk
1 egg, beaten
60ml/4 tbsp plain chocolate chips or
    chopped chocolate
Glossy Chocolate Sauce and whipped
    cream, to serve

1 Prepare a steamer or half fill a saucepan with water and bring it to the boil. Grease a 1 litre/1¾ pint/4 cup pudding basin. Sift the flour into a bowl and rub in the butter or margarine until the mixture resembles breadcrumbs.

2 Mash the bananas in a bowl. Stir them into the creamed mixture, with the caster sugar.

3 Whisk the milk with the egg in a jug or bowl, then beat into the pudding mixture. Stir in the chocolate chips or chopped chocolate.

4 Spoon the mixture into the prepared basin, cover closely with a double thickness of foil, and steam for 2 hours, topping up the water as required during cooking.

5 Run a knife around the top of the pudding to loosen it, then turn it out on to a warm serving dish. Serve hot, with the chocolate sauce and a spoonful of whipped cream.

COOK'S TIP

If you have a food processor, make a quick-mix version by processing all the ingredients, except the chocolate, until smooth. Stir in the chocolate and proceed as in the recipe.

Hot Plum Batter Pudding

*Other fruits can be used in place of
plums, depending on the season.
Canned black cherries are a
convenient substitute to keep in the
storecupboard.*

INGREDIENTS

Serves 4

450g/1lb ripe red plums, quartered and
    stoned
200ml/7fl oz/⅞ cup skimmed milk
60ml/4 tbsp skimmed milk powder
15ml/1 tbsp light muscovado sugar
5ml/1 tsp vanilla essence
75g/3oz/⅔ cup self-raising flour
2 egg whites
icing sugar, to sprinkle

1 Preheat the oven to 220°C/
425°F/Gas 7. Lightly oil a wide,
shallow ovenproof dish and add
the plums.

2 Pour the milk, milk powder,
sugar, vanilla, flour and egg
whites into a blender or food
processor. Process until smooth.

3 Pour the batter over the plums.
Bake for 25–30 minutes, or
until puffed and golden. Sprinkle
with icing sugar and serve
immediately.

COOK'S TIP

If you don't have a food
processor, then place the dry
ingredients for the batter in a
large bowl and gradually whisk
in the milk and egg whites.

Glazed Apricot Sponge

*Proper puddings can be very high in
saturated fat, but this healthy
version uses the minimum of oil and
no eggs.*

INGREDIENTS

Serves 4

10ml/2 tsp golden syrup
411g/14½oz can apricot halves in fruit
    juice
150g/5oz/1¼ cups self-raising flour
75g/3oz/1½ cups fresh breadcrumbs
90g/3½oz/½ cup light muscovado sugar
5ml/1 tsp ground cinnamon
30ml/2 tbsp sunflower oil
175ml/6fl oz/¾ cup skimmed milk

1 Preheat the oven to 180°C/
350°F/Gas 4. Lightly oil a
900ml/1½ pint/3¾ cup pudding
basin. Spoon in the syrup.

2 Drain the apricots and reserve
the juice. Arrange about
8 halves in the basin. Purée the rest
of the apricots with the juice and
set aside.

3 Mix the flour, breadcrumbs,
sugar and cinnamon then beat
in the oil and milk. Spoon into the
basin and bake for 50–55 minutes,
or until firm and golden. Turn out
and serve with the puréed fruit as
an accompaniment.

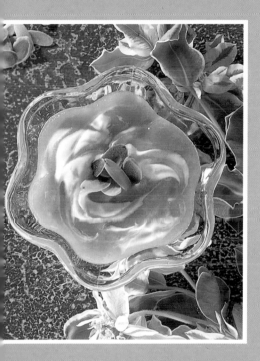

QUICK AND EASY

Frudités with Honey Dip

A colourful and tasty variation on the popular savoury crudités.

INGREDIENTS

Serves 4

225g/8oz/1 cup Greek-style yogurt

45ml/3 tbsp clear honey

selection of fresh fruit for dipping such as apples, pears, tangerines, grapes, figs, cherries, strawberries and kiwi fruit

1 Place the yogurt in a dish, beat until smooth, then partially stir in the honey, leaving a little marbled effect.

2 Cut the various fruits into wedges or bite-sized pieces or leave whole.

3 Arrange the fruits on a platter with the bowl of dip in the centre. Serve chilled.

COOK'S TIP

Sprinkle the apple and pear wedges with lemon juice to prevent discolouring.

Watermelon, Ginger and Grapefruit Salad

This pretty, pink combination is very light and refreshing for any summer meal.

INGREDIENTS

Serves 4

500g/1lb/2 cups diced watermelon flesh

2 ruby or pink grapefruit

2 pieces stem ginger in syrup

30ml/2 tbsp stem ginger syrup

whipped cream, to serve

1 Remove any seeds from the watermelon and cut into bite-sized chunks.

2 Using a small sharp knife, cut away all the peel and white pith from the grapefruit and carefully lift out the segments, catching any juice in a bowl.

COOK'S TIP

Toss the fruits gently – grapefruit segments will break up easily and the appearance of the dish will be spoiled.

3 Finely chop the stem ginger and place in a serving bowl with the melon cubes and grapefruit segments, adding the reserved juice.

4 Spoon over the ginger syrup and toss the fruits lightly to mix evenly. Chill before serving with a bowl of whipped cream.

Figs with Ricotta Cream

Fresh, ripe figs are full of natural sweetness, and need little adornment. This simple recipe makes the most of their beautiful, intense flavour.

INGREDIENTS

Serves 4

4 ripe, fresh figs

115g/4oz/½ cup ricotta or cottage cheese

45ml/3 tbsp crème fraîche

15ml/1 tbsp clear honey

2.5ml/½ tsp vanilla essence

freshly grated nutmeg, to decorate

3 Mix together the ricotta or cottage cheese, crème fraîche, honey and vanilla.

4 Spoon a little ricotta cream on to each plate and sprinkle with grated nutmeg to serve.

1 Trim the stalks from the figs. Make four cuts through each fig from the stalk-end, cutting them almost through but leaving them joined at the base.

2 Place the figs on serving plates and open them out.

Three-fruits Compote

Mixing dried fruits with fresh ones makes a good combination, especially if flavoured delicately with a little orange flower water. A melon-ball scoop gives the compote a classy touch, but you could chop the melon into cubes.

INGREDIENTS

Serves 6

175g/6oz/¾ cup no-need-to-soak, dried
  apricots
1 small ripe pineapple
1 small ripe melon
15ml/1 tbsp orange flower water
sprig of mint, to decorate

1 Put the apricots into a saucepan with 300ml/½ pint/1¼ cups of water. Bring to the boil, then simmer for 5 minutes. Set aside to cool.

2 Peel and quarter the pineapple then cut the core from each quarter and discard. Cut the flesh into chunks.

3 Seed the melon and scoop balls from the flesh. Save any juices which fall from the fruits and tip them into the apricots.

4 Stir in the orange flower water and mix all the fruits together. Pour into a serving dish, decorate with mint and chill lightly.

VARIATION

A good fruit salad needn't be a boring mixture of multi-coloured fruits swimming in sweet syrup. Instead of the usual apple, orange and grape type of salad, give it a theme, such as red berry fruits or a variety of sliced green fruits – even a dish of just one fruit nicely prepared and sprinkled lightly with some sugar and fresh lemon juice can look beautiful and tastes delicious. Do not use more than three fruits in a salad so that the flavours remain distinct.

Prune and Orange Pots

A simple, storecupboard dessert, made in minutes. It can be served straight away, but it's best chilled for about half an hour before serving.

Serves 4

225g/8oz/1 cup ready-to-eat dried prunes
150ml/¼ pint/⅔ cup orange juice
225g/8oz/1 cup low-fat natural yogurt
shreds of orange rind, to decorate

1 Remove the stones from the prunes and roughly chop them. Place them in a pan with the orange juice.

2 Bring the juice to the boil, stirring. Reduce the heat, cover and leave to simmer for 5 minutes, until the prunes are tender and the liquid is reduced by half.

3 Remove from the heat, allow to cool slightly and then beat well with a wooden spoon, until the fruit breaks down to a rough purée.

4 Transfer the mixture to a bowl. Stir in the yogurt, swirling the yogurt and fruit purée together lightly, to give an attractive marbled effect.

5 Spoon the mixture into stemmed glasses or individual dishes, smoothing the tops.

6 Top each dish with a few shreds of orange rind, to decorate. Chill before serving.

VARIATION

This dessert can also be made with other ready-to-eat dried fruit, such as apricots or peaches. For a special occasion, add a dash of brandy or Cointreau with the yogurt.

Quick Apricot Blender Whip

One of the quickest desserts you could make – as well as being one of the prettiest.

INGREDIENTS

Serves 4

400g/14oz can apricot halves in juice
15ml/1 tbsp Grand Marnier or brandy
175g/6oz/¾ cup Greek-style yogurt
30ml/2 tbsp flaked almonds

1 Drain the juice from the apricots and place the fruit and liqueur in a blender or food processor.

2 Process the apricots to a smooth purée.

3 Spoon the fruit purée and yogurt in alternate spoonfuls into four tall glasses or glass dishes, swirling them together slightly to give a marbled effect.

4 Lightly toast the almonds until they are golden. Let them cool slightly and then sprinkle them over the top.

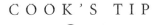

COOK'S TIP

For an even lighter dessert, use low-fat instead of Greek yogurt, and a little fruit juice from the can instead of liqueur.

Raspberry and Passion Fruit Swirls

If passion fruit is not available, this simple dessert can be made with raspberries alone.

INGREDIENTS

Serves 4

300g/11oz/scant 2 cups raspberries

2 passion fruit

400g/14oz/1⅔ cups low-fat fromage frais

30ml/2 tbsp granulated sugar

raspberries and sprigs of mint, to decorate

1 Mash the raspberries in a small bowl with a fork until the juice runs. Scoop out the passion fruit pulp into a separate bowl with the fromage frais and sugar and mix together thoroughly.

COOK'S TIP

Over-ripe, slightly soft fruit can also be used in this recipe. You could use frozen raspberries when fresh are not available, but thaw them first.

2 Spoon alternate spoonfuls of the raspberry pulp and the fromage frais mixture into stemmed glasses or one large serving dish, stirring lightly to create a swirled effect.

3 Decorate each dessert with a whole raspberry and a sprig of fresh mint. Serve chilled.

VARIATION

Other summer fruits would be just as delicious – try a mix of strawberries and redcurrants with the raspberries, or use mangoes, peaches or apricots, which you will need to purée in a food processor or blender before mixing with the fromage frais.

Raspberry Muesli Layer

As well as being a delicious, low-fat, high-fibre dessert, this can also be served for a quick, healthy breakfast.

INGREDIENTS

Serves 4

225g/8oz/1⅓ cups fresh or frozen and thawed raspberries
225g/8oz/1 cup low-fat natural yogurt
75g/3oz/¾ cup Swiss-style muesli

1 Reserve four raspberries for decoration, and then spoon a few raspberries into four stemmed glasses or glass dishes.

2 Top the raspberries with a spoonful of yogurt in each glass.

3 Sprinkle a generous layer of muesli over the yogurt.

4 Repeat with the raspberries and other ingredients. Top each with a whole raspberry.

COOK'S TIP

This recipe can be made in advance and stored in the fridge for several hours, or overnight if you're serving it for breakfast.

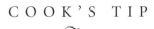

Almost Instant Banana Pudding

Banana and ginger make a great combination in this very fast dessert.

INGREDIENTS

Serves 6–8

4 thick slices ginger cake

6 bananas

30ml/2 tbsp lemon juice

300ml/½ pint/1¼ cups whipping cream or fromage frais

60ml/4 tbsp fruit juice

30–45ml/2–3 tbsp soft brown sugar

1 Break up the cake into chunks and arrange in an ovenproof dish. Slice the bananas and toss in the lemon juice.

2 Whip the cream and, when firm, gently whip in the juice. (If using fromage frais, just gently stir in the juice.) Fold in the bananas and spoon the mixture over the ginger cake.

3 Top with the soft brown sugar and place under a hot grill for 2–3 minutes to caramelize. Chill to set firm again if you wish, or serve when required.

Ginger and Orange Crème Brûlée

This is a useful way of cheating at crème brûlée! Most people would never know unless you overchill the custard or keep it more than a day, but there's little risk of that!

INGREDIENTS

Serves 4–5

2 eggs, plus 2 egg yolks

300ml/½ pint/1¼ cups single cream

30ml/2 tbsp caster sugar

5ml/1 tsp powdered gelatine or alternative

finely grated rind and juice of ½ orange

1 large piece stem ginger, finely chopped

45–60ml/3–4 tbsp icing or caster sugar

orange segments and sprig of mint, to decorate

COOK'S TIP

For a milder ginger flavour, just add up to 5ml/1 tsp ground ginger instead of the stem ginger.

---

1 Whisk the eggs and yolks together until pale. Bring the cream and sugar to the boil, remove from the heat and sprinkle on the gelatine. Stir until the gelatine has dissolved and then pour the cream mixture on to the eggs, whisking all the time.

2 Add the orange rind, a little juice to taste, and the chopped ginger to the mixture.

3 Pour into four or five ramekins and chill until set.

4 Some time before serving, sprinkle the sugar generously over the top of the custard and put under a very hot grill. Watch closely for the couple of moments it takes for the tops to caramelize. Allow to cool before serving. Decorate with a few segments of orange and a sprig of mint.

Pineapple Flambé

Flambéing means adding alcohol and then burning it off so the flavour is not too overpowering. This recipe is just as good, however, without the brandy – perfect if you wish to serve it to young children.

INGREDIENTS

Serves 4

1 large, ripe pineapple
40g/1½oz/3 tbsp unsalted butter
40g/1½oz/3 tbsp brown sugar
60ml/4 tbsp fresh orange juice
30ml/2 tbsp brandy or vodka
25g/1oz/4 tbsp slivered almonds, toasted

1 Cut away the top and base of the pineapple. Then cut down the sides, removing all the dark "eyes", but leaving the pineapple in a good shape.

2 Cut the pineapple into thin slices and, with an apple corer, remove the hard central core.

3 In a large frying pan melt the butter, sugar and orange juice. Add the pineapple slices and cook for about 1–2 minutes, turning once to coat both sides.

4 Add the brandy or vodka and light with a match immediately. Let the flames die down and then sprinkle with the toasted almonds.

Warm Pears in Cider

This is an excellent pudding for an autumn day.

INGREDIENTS

Serves 4

1 lemon
50g/2oz/¼ cup caster sugar
a little grated nutmeg
250ml/8fl oz/1 cup sweet cider
4 firm, ripe pears
freshly made custard, cream or ice cream, to serve

1 Carefully remove the rind from the lemon with a potato peeler leaving any white pith behind.

2 Squeeze the juice from the lemon into a saucepan, add the rind, sugar, nutmeg and cider and heat through to dissolve the sugar.

3 Carefully peel the pears, leaving the stalks on if possible, and place them in the pan of cider. Poach the pears for 10–15 minutes until almost tender, turning them frequently to cook evenly.

4 Transfer the pears to individual serving dishes using a slotted spoon. Simmer the liquid over a high heat until it reduces slightly and becomes syrupy.

5 Pour the warm syrup over the pears, and serve at once with freshly made custard, cream or ice cream.

COOK'S TIP

To get pears of just the right firmness, you may have to buy them slightly under-ripe and then wait a day or more. Soft pears are no good at all for this dish.

Chocolate Fudge Sundaes

They look impressive, taste fantastic and only take minutes to make.

INGREDIENTS

Serves 4

4 scoops each vanilla and coffee ice cream
2 small ripe bananas, sliced
whipped cream
toasted flaked almonds

For the sauce

50g/2oz/¼ cup soft light brown sugar
120ml/4fl oz/½ cup golden syrup
45ml/3 tbsp strong black coffee
5ml/1 tsp ground cinnamon
150g/5oz plain chocolate, chopped
85ml/3fl oz/⅓ cup whipping cream
45ml/3 tbsp coffee liqueur (optional)

1 To make the sauce, place the sugar, syrup, coffee and cinnamon in a heavy-based saucepan. Bring to the boil, then boil for about 5 minutes, stirring the mixture constantly.

2 Turn off the heat and stir in the chocolate. When melted and smooth, stir in the cream and liqueur, if using. Leave the sauce to cool slightly. If made ahead, reheat the sauce gently until just warm.

3 Fill four glasses with one scoop of vanilla and another of coffee ice cream.

4 Scatter the sliced bananas over the ice cream. Pour the warm fudge sauce over the bananas, then top each sundae with a generous swirl of whipped cream. Sprinkle toasted almonds over the cream and serve at once.

VARIATION

Ring the changes by choosing other flavours of ice cream such as strawberry, toffee or chocolate. In the summer, substitute raspberries or strawberries for the bananas, and scatter chopped roasted hazelnuts on top in place of the flaked almonds.

Brazilian Coffee Bananas

Rich, lavish and sinful-looking, this dessert takes only about two minutes to make!

INGREDIENTS

Serves 4

4 small ripe bananas

15ml/1 tbsp instant coffee granules or powder

30ml/2 tbsp dark muscovado sugar

250g/9oz/1⅛ cups Greek-style yogurt

15ml/1 tbsp toasted flaked almonds

1 Peel and slice one banana and mash the remaining three with a fork.

2 Dissolve the coffee in 15ml/ 1 tbsp of hot water and stir into the mashed bananas.

3 Spoon a little of the mashed banana mixture into four serving dishes and sprinkle with sugar. Top with a spoonful of yogurt, then repeat until all the ingredients are used up.

4 Swirl the last layer of yogurt for a marbled effect. Finish with a few banana slices and flaked almonds. Serve cold. Best eaten within about an hour of making.

VARIATION

For a special occasion, add a dash of dark rum or brandy to the bananas for extra richness.

Orange Yogurt Brûlées

A luxurious treat, but one that is much lower in fat than the classic brûlées, which are made with cream, eggs and lots of sugar.

INGREDIENTS

Serves 4

2 medium oranges

150g/5oz/⅔ cup Greek-style yogurt

50g/2oz/¼ cup crème fraîche

45ml/3 tbsp golden caster sugar

30ml/2 tbsp light muscovado sugar

1 With a sharp knife, cut away all the peel and white pith from the oranges and chop the fruit. Or, if there's time, segment the oranges, carefully removing all the membrane.

2 Place the fruit in the bottom of four individual flameproof dishes. Mix together the yogurt and crème fraîche and spoon the mixture over the oranges.

3 Mix together the two sugars and sprinkle them evenly over the tops of the dishes.

4 Place the dishes under a preheated, very hot grill for 3–4 minutes or until the sugar melts and turns into a rich golden brown. Serve warm or cold.

Grilled Pineapple with Rum Custard

Freshly ground black pepper may seem an unusual ingredient to put with pineapple, until you realise that peppercorns are the fruit of a tropical vine. If the idea does not appeal, leave out the pepper.

INGREDIENTS

Serves 4

1 ripe pineapple
25g/1oz/2tbsp butter
fresh strawberries, sliced, to serve
a few pineapple leaves, to decorate

For the sauce
1 egg
2 egg yolks
30ml/2 tbsp caster sugar
30ml/2 tbsp dark rum
2.5ml/½ tsp freshly ground black pepper

1 Remove the top and bottom from the pineapple with a serrated knife. Pare away the outer skin from top to bottom, remove the core and cut into slices.

2 Preheat a moderate grill. Dot the pineapple slices with butter and grill for about 5 minutes.

3 To make the sauce, place all the ingredients in a bowl. Set over a saucepan of simmering water and whisk with a hand-held mixer for about 3–4 minutes or until foamy and cooked. Scatter the strawberries over the pineapple, decorate with a few pineapple leaves and serve with the sauce.

COOK'S TIP

The sweetest pineapples are picked and exported when ripe. Contrary to popular belief, pineapples do not ripen well after picking. Choose fruit that smells sweet and yields to firm pressure from your thumbs.

Banana and Passion Fruit Whip

This very easy and quickly prepared dessert is delicious served with crisp shortcake or ginger biscuits.

INGREDIENTS

Serves 4

2 ripe bananas

2 passion fruit

90ml/6 tbsp fromage frais

150ml/¼ pint/⅔ cup double cream

10ml/2 tsp clear honey

shortcake or ginger biscuits, to serve

1 Peel the bananas, then mash them with a fork in a bowl to a smooth purée.

2 Halve the passion fruit and scoop out the pulp. Mix with the bananas and fromage frais. Whip the cream with the honey until it forms soft peaks.

3 Carefully fold the cream and honey mixture into the fruit mixture. Spoon into four glass dishes and serve at once with shortcake or ginger biscuits.

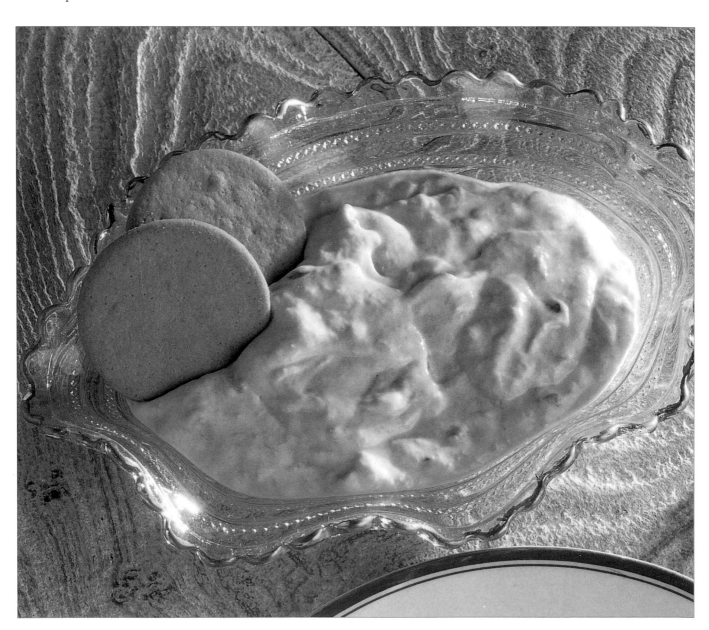

Cinnamon and Apricot Soufflés

Don't expect this to be difficult just because it's a soufflé – it really couldn't be easier, and, best of all, it's very low in calories.

Serves 4

3 eggs

115g/4oz/½ cup apricot fruit spread

finely grated rind of ½ lemon

5ml/1 tsp ground cinnamon

extra cinnamon, to decorate

1 Preheat the oven to 190°C/375°F/Gas 5. Lightly grease four individual soufflé dishes and dust them lightly with flour.

2 Separate the eggs and place the yolks in a bowl with the fruit spread, lemon rind and cinnamon.

3 Whisk hard until the mixture is thick and pale in colour.

4 Place the egg whites in a clean bowl and whisk them until they form soft peaks.

5 Using a metal spoon or spatula, fold the egg whites evenly into the yolk mixture.

6 Divide the soufflé mixture between the prepared dishes and bake for 10–15 minutes, until well-risen and golden brown. Serve immediately, dusted with a little extra ground cinnamon.

LOW
CALORIE

Fresh Citrus Jelly

Fresh fruit jellies really are worth the effort – they're packed with fresh flavour, natural colour and vitamins – and they make a lovely fat-free dessert.

INGREDIENTS

Serves 4

3 medium oranges

1 lemon

1 lime

75g/3oz/⅓ cup golden caster sugar

15ml/1 tbsp/1 sachet powdered gelatine, or alternative

extra slices of fruit, to decorate

1 With a sharp knife, cut all the peel and white pith from one orange and carefully remove the segments. Arrange the segments in the base of a 900ml/1½ pint/ 3¾ cup mould or dish.

2 Remove some shreds of citrus rind with a zester and reserve them for decoration. Grate the remaining rind from the lemon and lime and one orange. Place all the grated rind in a pan, with the sugar and 300ml/½ pint/1¼ cups of water.

3 Heat gently until the sugar has dissolved, without boiling. Remove from the heat. Squeeze the juice from all the rest of the fruit and stir it into the pan.

4 Strain the liquid into a measuring jug to remove the rind (you should have about 600ml/1 pint/2½ cups: if necessary, make up the amount with water). Sprinkle the gelatine over the liquid and stir until it has completely dissolved.

5 Pour a little of the jelly over the orange segments and chill until set. Leave the remaining jelly at room temperature to cool, but do not allow it to set.

6 Pour the remaining cooled jelly into the dish and chill until set. To serve, turn out the jelly and decorate it with the reserved citrus rind shreds and slices of citrus fruit.

Mandarins in Orange Flower Syrup

Mandarins, tangerines, clementines, mineolas: any of these lovely citrus fruits are suitable for this recipe.

INGREDIENTS

Serves 4

10 mandarins
15ml/1 tbsp icing sugar
10ml/2 tsp orange flower water
15ml/1 tbsp chopped pistachio nuts

1 Thinly pare a little of the coloured rind from one mandarin and cut it into fine shreds for decoration. Squeeze the juice from two mandarins and reserve it.

2 Peel the remaining fruit, removing as much of the white pith as possible. Arrange the whole fruits in a wide dish.

3 Mix the reserved juice, sugar and orange flower water and pour it over the fruit. Cover the dish and chill for at least 1 hour.

4 Blanch the shreds of rind in boiling water for 30 seconds. Drain, leave to cool and sprinkle them over the mandarins, with the pistachio nuts, to serve.

COOK'S TIP

The mandarins look very attractive if you leave them whole, especially if there is a large quantity for a special occasion, but you may prefer to separate the segments.

Minted Raspberry Bavarois

A sophisticated dessert that can be made a day in advance for a special dinner party.

INGREDIENTS

Serves 6

450g/1lb/2⅔ cups fresh or frozen and
    thawed raspberries

30ml/2 tbsp icing sugar

30ml/2 tbsp lemon juice

15ml/1 tbsp finely chopped fresh mint

30ml/2 tbsp/2 sachets powdered gelatine,
    or alternative

300ml/½ pint/1¼ cups custard, made with
    skimmed milk

250g/9oz/1⅛ cups Greek-style yogurt

fresh mint sprigs, to decorate

1 Reserve a few raspberries for decoration. Place the raspberries, icing sugar and lemon juice in a blender or food processor and process them until smooth.

2 Press the purée through a sieve to remove the raspberry pips. Add the mint. You should have about 600ml/1 pint/2½ cups of purée.

3 Sprinkle 5ml/1 tsp of the gelatine over 30ml/2 tbsp of boiling water and stir until the gelatine has dissolved. Stir into 150ml/¼ pint/⅔ cup of the fruit purée.

4 Pour this jelly into a 1 litre/ 1¾ pint/4 cup mould, and leave the mould to chill in the fridge until the jelly is just on the point of setting. Tip the tin to swirl the setting jelly around the sides, and then leave to chill until the jelly has set completely.

5 Stir the remaining fruit purée into the custard and yogurt. Dissolve the rest of the gelatine in 45ml/3 tbsp of boiling water and stir it in quickly.

6 Pour the raspberry custard into the mould and leave it to chill until it has set completely. To serve, dip the mould quickly into hot water and then turn it out and decorate it with the reserved raspberries and the mint sprigs.

Fruited Rice Ring

This unusual rice pudding looks beautiful turned out of a ring mould but if you prefer, stir the fruit into the rice and serve the dessert in individual dishes.

INGREDIENTS

Serves 4

65g/2½oz/5 tbsp short grain rice

900ml/1½ pint/3¾ cups semi-skimmed milk

1 cinnamon stick

175g/6oz/1 cup mixed dried fruit

175ml/6fl oz/¾ cup orange juice

45ml/3 tbsp caster sugar

finely grated rind of 1 small orange

1 Place the rice, milk and cinnamon stick in a large pan and bring to the boil. Cover and simmer, stirring occasionally, for about 1½ hours, until no free liquid remains.

2 Meanwhile, place the fruit and orange juice in a pan and bring to the boil. Cover and simmer very gently for about 1 hour, until tender and no free liquid remains.

3 Remove the cinnamon stick from the rice and stir in the sugar and orange rind.

4 Tip the fruit into the base of a lightly oiled 1.5 litre/2½ pint/ 6¼ cup ring mould. Spoon the rice over, smoothing down firmly. Chill until needed.

5 Run a knife around the edge of the mould and turn out the rice carefully on to a serving plate.

Apple Foam with Blackberries

This light dessert provides a good contrast in flavour, text and colour.

INGREDIENTS

Serves 4

225g/8oz blackberries

150ml/¼ pint/⅔ cup apple juice

5ml/1 tsp powdered gelatine

15ml/1 tbsp clear honey

2 egg whites

1 Place the blackberries in a pan with 60ml/4 tbsp of the apple juice and heat gently until the fruit is soft. Remove from the heat, cool and chill.

2 Sprinkle the gelatine over the remaining apple juice in another pan and stir over a low heat until dissolved. Stir in the honey.

3 Whisk the egg whites in a bowl until they hold stiff peaks. Continue whisking hard and pour in the hot gelatine mixture gradually, until well mixed.

4 Quickly spoon the foam into rough mounds on individual plates. Chill. Serve with the blackberries and juice spooned around.

VARIATION

Any seasonal soft fruit can be used to accompany the apple if blackberries are not available.

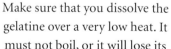

COOK'S TIP

Make sure that you dissolve the gelatine over a very low heat. It must not boil, or it will lose its setting ability.

Cappuccino Coffee Cups

Coffee-lovers will love this one – and it tastes rich and creamy, even though it's very light.

Serves 4

2 eggs

215g/7.7oz carton evaporated semi-skimmed milk

25ml/1½ tbsp instant coffee granules or powder

30ml/2 tbsp caster sugar

10ml/2 tsp powdered gelatine, or alternative

60ml/4 tbsp light crème fraîche

cocoa powder or ground cinnamon, to decorate

1 Separate one egg and reserve the white. Beat the yolk with the whole of the remaining egg.

2 Put the evaporated milk, coffee granules, sugar and beaten eggs in a pan; whisk until evenly combined.

3 Put the pan over a low heat and stir constantly until the mixture is hot, but not boiling. Cook, stirring constantly, without boiling, until the mixture is slightly thickened and smooth.

4 Remove the pan from the heat. Sprinkle the gelatine over the pan and whisk until the gelatine has completely dissolved.

5 Spoon the coffee custard into four individual dishes or glasses and chill them until set.

6 Whisk the reserved egg white until stiff. Whisk in the crème fraîche and then spoon the mixture over the desserts. Sprinkle with cocoa or cinnamon and serve.

VARIATION

Greek-style yogurt can be used instead of the crème fraîche, if you prefer.

Summer Fruit Salad Ice Cream

What could be more cooling on a hot day than fresh summer fruits, lightly frozen in this irresistible ice?

INGREDIENTS

Serves 6

900g/2lb/5 cups mixed soft summer fruit, such as raspberries, strawberries, black-currants, redcurrants, etc.

2 eggs

225g/8oz/1 cup Greek-style yogurt

175ml/6fl oz/¾ cup red grape juice

15ml/1 tbsp/1 sachet powdered gelatine, or alternative

4 Whisk the dissolved gelatine mixture into the fruit purée and then pour the mixture into a freezer container. Freeze until half-frozen and slushy in consistency.

5 Whisk the egg whites until they are stiff. Quickly fold them into the half-frozen mixture.

6 Return to the freezer and freeze until almost firm. Scoop into individual dishes or glasses and add the reserved soft fruits.

1 Reserve half the fruit and purée the rest in a blender or food processor, or rub it through a sieve to make a smooth purée.

2 Separate the eggs and whisk the yolks and the yogurt into the fruit purée.

3 Heat the grape juice until it's almost boiling, then remove it from the heat. Sprinkle the gelatine over the juice and stir to dissolve the gelatine completely.

Plum and Port Sorbet

Rather a grown-up sorbet, this one, but you could use fresh, still red grape juice in place of the port if you wished to leave out the alcohol.

INGREDIENTS

Serves 4–6

900g/2lb ripe red plums, halved
    and stoned
75g/3oz/6 tbsp caster sugar
45ml/3 tbsp ruby port or red wine
crisp biscuits, to serve (optional)

1 Place the plums in a pan with the sugar and 45ml/3 tbsp water. Stir over a low heat until the sugar is melted, then cover and simmer gently for about 5 minutes, until the fruit is soft.

2 Turn into a blender or food processor and purée until smooth, then stir in the port. Cool completely, then tip into a freezer container and freeze until firm round the edges.

3 Spoon into the food processor and process until smooth. Return to the freezer and freeze until solid.

4 Allow to soften slightly at room temperature for 15–20 minutes before serving in scoops, with sweet biscuits.

Tofu Berry "Cheesecake"

This summery "cheesecake" is a very light and refreshing finish to any meal. Strictly speaking, it is not a cheesecake at all, as it's based on tofu – but who would guess?

INGREDIENTS

Serves 6

50g/2oz/4 tbsp low-fat spread

30ml/2 tbsp apple juice

115g/4oz/6 cups bran flakes or other high-fibre cereal

For the filling

275g/10oz/1¼ cups tofu or skimmed-milk soft cheese

200g/7oz/⅞ cup low-fat natural yogurt

15ml/1 tbsp/1 sachet powdered gelatine

60ml/4 tbsp apple juice

For the topping

175g/6oz/1¾ cups mixed summer soft fruit, e.g. strawberries, raspberries, red-currants, blackberries, etc. (or frozen "fruits of the forest")

30ml/2 tbsp redcurrant jelly

1 For the base, place the low-fat spread and apple juice in a pan and heat them gently until the spread has melted. Crush the cereal and stir it into the pan.

2 Tip into a 23cm/9in round flan tin and press down firmly. Leave to set.

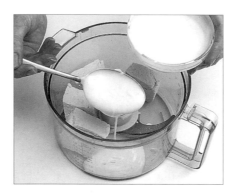

3 For the filling, place the tofu or cheese and yogurt in a blender or food processor and process them until smooth. Dissolve the gelatine in the apple juice and stir the juice immediately into the tofu mixture.

4 Spread the tofu mixture over the chilled base, smoothing it evenly. Place in the fridge until the filling has set.

5 Remove the flan tin and place the "cheesecake" on a serving plate.

6 Arrange the fruits over the top. Melt the redcurrant jelly with 30ml/2 tbsp hot water. Let it cool, then spoon over the fruit to serve.

COOK'S TIP

The lowest-calorie breakfast cereals are usually those which are highest in fibre, so it is worth checking the labels for comparisons.

Floating Islands in Hot Plum Sauce

A low-fat version of the French classic, that is simpler to make than it looks. The plum sauce can be made in advance, and reheated just before you cook the meringues.

INGREDIENTS

Serves 4

450g/1lb red plums

300ml/½ pint/1¼ cups apple juice

2 egg whites

30ml/2 tbsp concentrated apple
   juice syrup

freshly grated nutmeg, to serve

1 Halve the plums and remove the stones. Place them in a wide pan, with the apple juice.

2 Bring to the boil and then cover with a lid and leave to simmer gently for 20–30 minutes or until the plums are tender.

3 Place the egg whites in a clean, dry bowl and whisk them until they hold soft peaks.

4 Gradually whisk in the apple juice syrup, whisking until the meringue holds fairly firm peaks.

5 Using a tablespoon, scoop the meringue mixture into the gently simmering plum sauce. You may need to cook the "islands" in two batches.

6 Cover and allow to simmer gently for 2–3 minutes, until the meringues are just set. Serve straight away, sprinkled with a little freshly grated nutmeg.

COOK'S TIP

A bottle of concentrated apple juice is a useful store cupboard sweetener, but if you don't have any, use a little honey instead.

Grilled Nectarines with Ricotta and Spice

This easy dessert is good at any time of year – use canned peach halves if fresh ones are not available.

INGREDIENTS

Serves 4

4 ripe nectarines or peaches

15ml/1 tbsp light muscovado sugar

115g/4oz/½ cup ricotta cheese or
   fromage frais

2.5ml/½ tsp ground star anise

1 Cut the nectarines in half and remove the stones.

2 Arrange the nectarines, cut-side upwards, in a wide flameproof dish or on a baking sheet.

3 Stir the sugar into the ricotta or fromage frais. Using a teaspoon, spoon the mixture into the hollow of each nectarine half.

4 Sprinkle with the star anise. Place under a moderately hot grill for 6–8 minutes, or until the nectarines are hot and bubbling. Serve warm.

COOK'S TIP

Star anise has a warm, rich flavour – if you can't get it, try ground cloves or ground mixed spice instead.

Chocolate Vanilla Timbales

The occasional chocolate treat doesn't do any harm, especially if it's a dessert as light as this one.

INGREDIENTS

Serves 6

350ml/12fl oz/1½ cups semi-skimmed milk

30ml/2 tbsp cocoa powder

2 eggs

5ml/1 tsp vanilla essence

45ml/3 tbsp caster sugar

15ml/1 tbsp/1 sachet powdered gelatine, or alternative

sprig of mint, to decorate

For the sauce

115g/4oz/½ cup light Greek-style yogurt

2.5ml/½ tsp vanilla essence

extra cocoa powder, to sprinkle

1 Place the milk and cocoa in a saucepan and stir until the milk is boiling. Separate the eggs and beat the egg yolks with the vanilla and sugar in a bowl, until the mixture is pale and smooth. Gradually pour in the chocolate milk, beating well.

2 Return the mixture to the pan and stir constantly over a gentle heat, without boiling, until it's slightly thickened and smooth. Dissolve the gelatine in 45ml/ 3 tbsp of hot water and then quickly stir it into the milk mixture. Let it cool until it's on the point of setting.

3 Whisk the egg whites until they hold soft peaks. Fold the egg whites quickly into the milk mixture. Spoon the timbale mixture into six individual moulds and chill them until set.

4 To serve, run a knife around the edge, dip the moulds quickly into hot water and turn out the chocolate timbales on to serving plates and decorate with a sprig of mint. For the sauce, stir together the yogurt and vanilla, spoon on to the plates and sprinkle with a little more cocoa powder.

Fluffy Banana and Pineapple Mousse

This light, low-fat mousse looks very impressive but is really very easy to make, especially with a food processor. To make it even simpler, use a 1 litre/1¾ pint/4 cup serving dish which will hold all the mixture without a paper "collar".

INGREDIENTS

Serves 6

2 ripe bananas

225g/8oz/1 cup cottage cheese

425g/15oz can pineapple chunks or pieces in juice

15ml/1 tbsp/1 sachet powdered gelatine, or alternative

2 egg whites

1 Tie a double band of non-stick baking paper around a 600ml/ 1 pint/2½ cup soufflé dish, to come 5cm/2in above the rim.

2 Peel and chop one banana and place it in a blender or food processor with the cottage cheese. Process them until smooth.

3 Drain the pineapple, reserving the juice, and reserve a few pieces or chunks for decoration. Add the rest to the mixture in the blender or processor and process for a few seconds until finely chopped.

4 Dissolve the gelatine in 60ml/ 4 tbsp of the reserved pineapple juice. Stir the gelatine quickly into the fruit mixture.

5 Whisk the egg whites until they hold soft peaks and fold them into the mixture. Tip the mousse mixture into the prepared dish, smooth the surface and chill, until set.

6 When the mousse is set, carefully remove the paper collar and decorate with the reserved banana and pineapple.

Greek Honey and Lemon Cake

The semolina in this recipe gives the cake an excellent texture.

Makes 16 slices

40g/1½oz/3 tbsp sunflower margarine

60ml/4 tbsp clear honey

finely grated rind and juice of 1 lemon

150ml/¼ pint/⅔ cup skimmed milk

150g/5oz/1¼ cups plain flour

7.5ml/1½ tsp baking powder

2.5ml/½ tsp grated nutmeg

50g/2oz/⅓ cup semolina

2 egg whites

10ml/2 tsp sesame seeds

1 Preheat the oven to 200°C/ 400°F/Gas 6. Lightly oil a 19cm/7½in square deep cake tin and line the base with non-stick baking paper.

2 Place the margarine and 45ml/3 tbsp of the honey in a saucepan and heat gently until melted. Reserve 15ml/1 tbsp lemon juice, then stir in the rest with the lemon rind and milk.

3 Stir together the flour, baking powder and nutmeg, then beat in with the semolina. Whisk the egg whites until they form soft peaks, then fold evenly into the semolina mixture.

4 Spoon into the tin and sprinkle with sesame seeds. Bake for 25–30 minutes, until golden brown.

5 Mix the reserved honey and lemon juice and drizzle over the cake while warm. Cool in the tin, then cut into fingers to serve.

Strawberry Roulade

An attractive and delicious cake, perfect for a family supper.

Serves 6

4 egg whites

115g/4oz/scant ⅔ cup golden caster sugar

75g/3oz/⅔ cup plain flour, sifted

30ml/2 tbsp orange juice

caster sugar, for sprinkling

115g/4oz/1 cup strawberries, chopped

150g/5oz/¾ cup low-fat fromage frais

strawberries, to decorate

1 Preheat the oven to 200°C/ 400°F/Gas 6. Oil a 23 x 33cm/ 9 x 13in Swiss roll tin and line with non-stick baking paper.

2 Place the egg whites in a large clean bowl and whisk until they form soft peaks. Gradually whisk in the sugar. Fold in half of the sifted flour, then fold in the rest with the orange juice.

3 Spoon the mixture into the prepared tin, spreading evenly. Bake for 15–18 minutes, or until it is golden brown and firm to the touch.

4 Meanwhile, spread out a sheet of non-stick baking paper and sprinkle with caster sugar. Turn out the cake on to this and remove the lining paper. Roll up the sponge loosely from one short side, with the paper inside. Cool.

5 Unroll and remove the paper. Stir the strawberries into the fromage frais and spread over the sponge. Roll up and serve decorated with strawberries.

Apricot and Orange Roulade

*This elegant dessert is very good
served with a spoonful of Greek-
style yogurt or crème fraîche.*

INGREDIENTS

Serves 6

4 egg whites

115g/4oz/scant ⅔ cup golden caster sugar

50g/2oz/½ cup plain flour

finely grated rind of 1 small orange

45ml/3 tbsp orange juice

For the filling

**115g/4oz/½ cup ready-to-eat dried
    apricots**

150ml/¼ pint/⅔ cup orange juice

10ml/2 tsp icing sugar, for sprinkling

shreds of orange zest, to decorate

1 Preheat the oven to
200°C/400°F/Gas 6. Grease a
23 x 33cm/9 x 13in Swiss roll tin
and line it with non-stick baking
paper. Grease the paper.

COOK'S TIP

Make and bake the sponge
mixture a day in advance and
keep it, rolled with the paper, in a
cool place. Fill it with the fruit
purée 2–3 hours before serving.
The sponge can also be frozen for
up to 2 months: thaw it at room
temperature and fill it as above.

2 To make the roulade, place the
egg whites in a large clean
bowl and whisk them until they
hold soft peaks. Gradually add the
sugar, whisking vigorously
between each addition.

3 Fold in the flour, orange rind
and juice. Spoon the mixture
into the prepared tin and spread
it evenly.

4 Bake for 15–18 minutes, or
until the sponge is firm and
light golden in colour. Turn out on
to a sheet of non-stick baking
paper and roll it up loosely from
one short side. Leave to cool.

5 Roughly chop the apricots and
place them in a pan, with the
orange juice. Cover the pan and
leave to simmer until most of the
liquid has been absorbed. Purée in
a blender or food processor.

6 Unroll the roulade and spread
with the apricot mixture. Roll
up, arrange strips of paper
diagonally across the roll, sprinkle
lightly with lines of icing sugar,
remove the paper and scatter with
orange zest to serve.

Filo Chiffon Pie

Filo pastry is low in fat and is very easy to use. Keep a pack in the freezer, ready to make impressive puddings like this one.

INGREDIENTS

Serves 3

500g/1¼lb pink rhubarb

5ml/1 tsp mixed spice

finely grated rind and juice of 1 orange

15ml/1 tbsp caster sugar

15g/½oz/1 tbsp butter

3 sheets filo pastry

1 Preheat the oven to 200°C/ 400°F/Gas 6. Trim the leaves and ends from the rhubarb sticks and chop them in 2.5cm/1in pieces. Place them in a bowl.

2 Add the mixed spice, orange rind and juice and sugar and toss well to coat evenly. Tip the rhubarb into a 1 litre/1¾ pint/ 4 cup pie dish.

3 Melt the butter and brush it over the pastry sheets. Lift the pastry sheets on to the pie dish, butter-side up, and crumple them to form a chiffon effect, covering the pie completely.

4 Place the dish on a baking sheet and bake it for 20 minutes, until golden brown. Reduce the heat to 180°C/350°F/ Gas 4 and bake for a further 10–15 minutes, until the rhubarb is tender. Serve warm.

VARIATION

Other fruit such as apples, pears or peaches can be used in this pie – try it with whatever is in season.

Crunchy Gooseberry Crumble

Gooseberries are perfect for traditional family puddings like this one. When they are out of season, other fruits such as apples, plums or rhubarb could be used instead.

Serves 4

500g/1¼lb/5 cups gooseberries

50g/2oz/4 tbsp caster sugar

75g/3oz/scant 1 cup rolled oats

75g/3oz/⅔ cup wholemeal flour

60ml/4 tbsp sunflower oil

50g/2oz/4 tbsp demerara sugar

30ml/2 tbsp chopped walnuts

natural yogurt or custard, to serve

1 Preheat the oven to 200°C/ 400°F/Gas 6. Place the gooseberries in a pan with the caster sugar. Cover the pan and cook over a low heat for 10 minutes, until the gooseberries are just tender. Tip into an ovenproof dish.

2 To make the crumble, place the oats, flour and oil in a bowl and stir with a fork until evenly mixed.

3 Stir in the demerara sugar and walnuts, then spread evenly over the gooseberries. Bake for 25–30 minutes, or until golden and bubbling. Serve hot with yogurt, or custard made with skimmed milk.

COOK'S TIP

❧

The best gooseberries to use for cooking are the early, small, firm green ones.

Spiced Date and Walnut Cake

A classic flavour combination, which makes a very easy low fat, high-fibre cake.

INGREDIENTS

Makes 1 cake

300g/11oz/2¾ cups wholemeal self-raising
  flour
10ml/2 tsp mixed spice
150g/5oz/1 cup chopped dates
50g/2oz/½ cup chopped walnuts
60ml/4 tbsp sunflower oil
115g/4oz/½ cup dark muscovado sugar
300ml/½ pint/1¼ cups skimmed milk
walnut halves, to decorate

1 Preheat the oven to 180°C/
350°F/Gas 4. Grease and line
a 900g/2lb loaf tin with greaseproof paper.

2 Sift together the flour and
spice, adding back any bran
from the sieve. Stir in the dates
and walnuts.

3 Mix the oil, sugar and milk,
then stir evenly into the dry
ingredients. Spoon into the
prepared tin and arrange the
walnut halves on top.

4 Bake the cake in the oven for
about 45–50 minutes, or until
golden brown and firm. Turn out
the cake, remove the lining paper
and leave to cool on a wire rack.

VARIATION

Pecan nuts can be used in place of
the walnuts in this cake.

Banana Orange Loaf

For the best banana flavour and a really good, moist texture, make sure the bananas are very ripe.

INGREDIENTS

Makes 1 loaf

90g/3½oz/generous ¾ cup wholemeal plain flour
90g/3½oz/generous ¾ cup plain flour
5ml/1 tsp baking powder
5ml/1 tsp ground mixed spice
45ml/3 tbsp flaked hazelnuts, toasted
2 large ripe bananas
1 egg
30ml/2 tbsp sunflower oil
30ml/2 tbsp clear honey
finely grated rind and juice of 1 small orange
4 orange slices, halved
10ml/2 tsp icing sugar

1 Preheat the oven to 180°C/ 350°F/Gas 4. Brush a 1 litre/ 1¾ pint/4 cup loaf tin with sunflower oil and line the base with non-stick baking paper.

2 Sift the flours with the baking powder and spice into a bowl.

3 Stir the hazelnuts into the dry ingredients. Peel and mash the bananas. Beat in the egg, oil, honey and the orange rind and juice. Stir evenly into the dry ingredients.

4 Spoon into the prepared tin and smooth the top. Bake for 40–45 minutes, or until firm and golden brown. Turn out and cool on a wire rack.

5 Sprinkle the orange slices with the icing sugar and grill until golden. Use to decorate the cake.

COOK'S TIP

If you plan to keep the loaf for more than two or three days, omit the orange slices. Brush the cake with honey and sprinkle with flaked hazelnuts.

Banana Ginger Parkin

Parkin improves with keeping. Store it in a covered container for up to two months.

INGREDIENTS

Makes 12 squares

200g/7oz/1¾ cups plain flour
10ml/2 tsp bicarbonate of soda
10ml/2 tsp ground ginger
150g/5oz/1¼ cups medium oatmeal
60ml/4 tbsp dark muscovado sugar
75g/3oz/6 tbsp sunflower margarine
150g/5oz/⅔ cup golden syrup
1 egg, beaten
3 ripe bananas, mashed
75g/3oz/¾ cup icing sugar
stem ginger, to decorate

1 Preheat the oven to 160°C/325°F/Gas 3. Grease and line an 18 x 28cm/7 x 11in cake tin.

2 Sift together the flour, bicarbonate of soda and ginger, then stir in the oatmeal. Melt the sugar, margarine and syrup in a saucepan, then stir into the flour mixture. Beat in the egg and mashed bananas.

3 Spoon into the tin and bake for about 1 hour, or until firm to the touch. Allow to cool in the tin, then turn out and cut into even-sized squares.

4 Sift the icing sugar into a bowl and stir in just enough water to make a smooth, runny icing. Drizzle the icing over each square and top with pieces of stem ginger, if you like.

COOK'S TIP
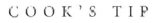
This is a nutritious cake, ideal for packed lunches as it doesn't break up too easily.

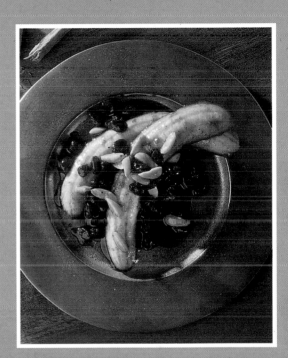

FRUIT
DESSERTS

~

Cherries Jubilee

Fresh cherries are wonderful cooked lightly to serve hot over ice cream. Children will love this dessert.

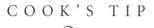
INGREDIENTS

Serves 4

450g/1lb red or black cherries

115g/4oz/generous ½ cup granulated sugar

pared rind of 1 lemon

15ml/1 tbsp arrowroot

60ml/4 tbsp Kirsch

vanilla ice cream, to serve

COOK'S TIP

If you don't have a cherry stoner, simply push the stones through with a skewer. Remember to save the juice to use in the recipe.

1 Stone the cherries over a pan to catch the juice. Drop the stones into the pan as you work.

2 Add the sugar, lemon rind and 300ml/½ pint/1¼ cups water to the pan. Stir over a low heat until the sugar dissolves, then bring to the boil and simmer for 10 minutes. Strain the syrup, then return to the pan. Add the cherries and cook for 3–4 minutes.

3 Blend the arrowroot to a paste with 15ml/1 tbsp cold water and stir into the cherries, after removing them from the heat.

4 Return the pan to the heat and bring to the boil, stirring all the time. Cook the sauce for a minute or two, stirring until it is thick and smooth. Heat the Kirsch in a ladle over a flame, ignite and pour over the cherries. Spoon the cherries and hot sauce over scoops of ice cream and serve at once.

Apricots in Marsala

Make sure the apricots are completely covered by the syrup so that they don't discolour.

INGREDIENTS

Serves 4

12 apricots

50g/2oz/4 tbsp caster sugar

300ml/½ pint/1¼ cups Marsala

2 strips pared orange rind

1 vanilla pod, split

150ml/¼ pint/⅔ cup double or whipping cream

15ml/1 tbsp icing sugar

1.5ml/¼ tsp ground cinnamon

150ml/¼ pint/⅔ cup Greek-style yogurt

1 Halve and stone the apricots, then place in a bowl of boiling water for about 30 seconds. Drain well, then slip off their skins.

2 Place the caster sugar, Marsala, orange rind, vanilla pod and 250ml/8fl oz/1 cup water in a pan. Heat gently until the sugar dissolves. Bring to the boil, without stirring, then simmer for 2–3 minutes.

3 Add the apricot halves to the pan and poach for 5–6 minutes, or until just tender. Using a slotted spoon, transfer the apricots to a serving dish.

4 Boil the syrup rapidly until reduced by half, then pour over the apricots and leave to cool. Cover and chill. Remove the orange rind and vanilla pod.

5 Whip the cream with the icing sugar and cinnamon until it forms soft peaks. Gently fold in the yogurt. Spoon into a serving bowl and chill. Serve with the apricots.

Poached Pears in Red Wine

This makes a very pretty dessert, as the pears take on a red blush from the wine.

INGREDIENTS

Serves 4

1 bottle red wine

150g/5oz/¾ cup caster sugar

45ml/3 tbsp honey

juice of ½ lemon

1 cinnamon stick

1 vanilla pod, split open lengthways

5cm/2in piece of orange rind

1 clove

1 black peppercorn

4 firm, ripe pears

whipped cream or soured cream, to serve

1 Place the wine, sugar, honey, lemon juice, cinnamon stick, vanilla pod, orange rind, clove and peppercorn in a saucepan just large enough to hold the pears standing upright. Heat gently, stirring occasionally until the sugar has completely dissolved.

2 Meanwhile, peel the pears, leaving the stem intact. Take a thin slice off the base of each pear so that it will stand square and upright in the pan.

3 Place the pears in the wine mixture, then simmer, uncovered, for 20–35 minutes depending on size and ripeness, until the pears are just tender; be careful not to overcook.

4 Carefully transfer the pears to a bowl using a slotted spoon. Continue to boil the poaching liquid until reduced by about half. Leave to cool, then strain the cooled liquid over the pears and chill for at least 3 hours.

5 Place the pears in four individual serving dishes and spoon over a little of the red wine syrup. Serve with whipped cream or soured cream.

Hot Bananas with Rum and Raisins

Choose almost-ripe bananas with evenly coloured skins, either all yellow or just green at the tips. Over-ripe bananas will not hold their shape so well when cooked.

INGREDIENTS

Serves 4

40g/1½oz/scant ¼ cup seedless raisins

75ml/5 tbsp dark rum

50g/2oz/4 tbsp unsalted butter

60ml/4 tbsp soft light brown sugar

4 ripe bananas, peeled and halved
    lengthways

1.5ml/¼ tsp grated nutmeg

1.5ml/¼ tsp ground cinnamon

30ml/2 tbsp slivered almonds, toasted

chilled cream or vanilla ice cream, to serve
    (optional)

1 Put the raisins in a bowl with the rum. Leave them to soak for about 30 minutes to plump up.

2 Melt the butter in a frying pan, add the sugar and stir until dissolved. Add the bananas and cook for a few minutes until they are tender.

3 Sprinkle the spices over the bananas, then pour in the rum and raisins. Carefully set alight using a long taper and stir gently to mix.

4 Scatter over the slivered almonds and serve immediately with chilled cream or vanilla ice cream, if you like.

Blueberry Pancakes

These are rather like the thick American breakfast pancakes – though they can, of course, be eaten at any time of the day.

INGREDIENTS

Makes 6–8

115g/4oz/1 cup self-raising flour
pinch of salt
45–60ml/3–4 tbsp caster sugar
2 eggs
120ml/4fl oz/½ cup milk
15–30ml/1–2 tbsp oil
115g/4oz/1 cup fresh or frozen
  blueberries, plus extra to decorate
maple syrup, to serve
lemon wedges, to decorate

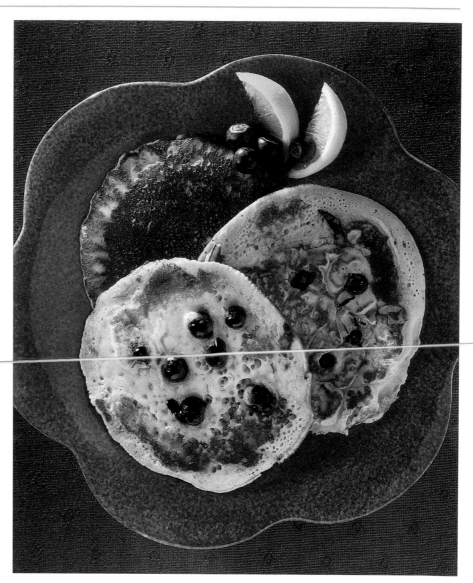

1 Sift the flour into a bowl with the salt and sugar. Beat together the eggs thoroughly. Make a well in the middle of the flour and stir in the eggs.

2 Gradually blend in a little of the milk to make a smooth batter. Then whisk in the rest of the milk and whisk for 1–2 minutes. Allow to rest for 20–30 minutes.

COOK'S TIP

Instead of blueberries you could use blackberries or raspberries. If you use canned fruit, make sure it is very well drained.

3 Heat a few drops of oil in a pancake pan or heavy-based frying pan until just hazy. Pour about 30ml/2 tbsp of the batter and swirl the batter around until it makes an even shape.

4 Cook for 2–3 minutes and when almost set on top, sprinkle over 15–30ml/1–2 tbsp blueberries. As soon as the base is loose and golden brown, turn the pancake over.

5 Cook on the second side for only about 1 minute, until golden and crisp. Slide the pancake on to a plate and serve drizzled with maple syrup. Continue with the rest of the batter. Serve decorated with lemon wedges and a few extra blueberries.

Rhubarb-Strawberry Crisp

Strawberries, cinnamon and ground almonds make this a luxurious and delicious version of rhubarb crumble.

INGREDIENTS

Serves 4

225g/8oz strawberries, hulled

450g/1lb rhubarb, diced

90g/3½oz/½ cup granulated sugar

15ml/1 tbsp cornflour

85ml/3fl oz/⅓ cup fresh orange juice

115g/4oz/1 cup plain flour

90g/3½oz/1 cup rolled oats

115g/4oz/½ cup light brown sugar, firmly packed

2.5ml/½ tsp ground cinnamon

50g/2oz/½ cup ground almonds

150g/5oz/generous ½ cup cold butter

1 egg, lightly beaten

1 If the strawberries are large, cut them in half. Combine the strawberries, rhubarb and granulated sugar in a 2.4 litre/ 4 pint/10 cup baking dish. Preheat the oven to 180°C/350°F/Gas 4.

2 In a small bowl, blend the cornflour with the orange juice. Pour this mixture over the fruit and stir gently to coat. Set the baking dish aside while making the crumble topping.

3 In a bowl, toss together the flour, oats, brown sugar, cinnamon and ground almonds. With a pastry blender or two knives, cut in the butter until the mixture resembles coarse bread-crumbs. Stir in the beaten egg.

4 Spoon the oat mixture evenly over the fruit and press down gently. Bake until browned, 50–60 minutes, then serve warm.

Mango Sorbet

A light and refreshing dessert that's surprisingly easy to make.

INGREDIENTS

Serves 6

150g/5oz/¾ cup caster sugar

a large strip of orange rind

1 large mango, peeled, stoned and cubed

60ml/4 tbsp orange juice

mint sprigs, to decorate

1 Combine the sugar, orange rind and 175ml/6fl oz/¾ cup water in a saucepan. Bring to the boil, stirring to dissolve the sugar. Leave the syrup to cool.

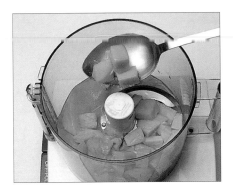

2 Purée the mango cubes with the orange juice in a blender or food processor. There should be about 475ml/16fl oz/2 cups of the purée.

3 Add the purée to the cooled sugar syrup and mix well. Strain, then chill.

4 When cold, tip into a freezer container and freeze until firm round the edges.

5 Spoon the semi-frozen mixture into the food processor and process until smooth. Return to the freezer and freeze until solid. Allow the sorbet to soften slightly at room temperature for 15–20 minutes before serving, decorated with mint sprigs.

VARIATIONS

For Banana Sorbet: peel and cube 4–5 large bananas. Purée with 30ml/2 tbsp lemon juice to make 475ml/16fl oz/2 cups. If liked, replace the orange rind in the sugar syrup with 2–3 whole cloves, or omit the rind.

For Paw Paw Sorbet: peel, seed and cube 675g/1½lb paw paw. Purée with 45ml/3 tbsp lime juice to make 475ml/16fl oz/2 cups. Replace the orange rind with lime rind.

For Passion Fruit Sorbet: halve 16 or more passion fruit and scoop out the seeds and pulp (there should be about 475ml/16fl oz/ 2 cups). Work in a blender or food processor until the seeds are like coarse pepper. Omit the orange juice and rind. Add the passion fruit to the sugar syrup, then press through a wire sieve before freezing.

Raspberry Trifle

Use fresh or frozen raspberries for this ever-popular desert.

INGREDIENTS

Serves 6 or more

175g/6oz trifle sponges or plain Victoria sponge, cut into 2.5cm/1in cubes , or coarsely crumbled sponge fingers

60ml/4 tbsp medium sherry

115g/4oz raspberry jam

275g/10oz/1⅔ cups raspberries

450ml/¾ pint/scant 2 cups custard, flavoured with 30ml/2 tbsp medium or sweet sherry

300ml/½ pint/1¼ cups sweetened whipped cream

toasted flaked almonds and mint leaves, to decorate

1 Spread half of the sponges, cake cubes or sponge fingers over the bottom of a large serving bowl. (A glass bowl is best for presentation.)

2 Sprinkle half of the sherry over the cake to moisten it. Spoon over half of the jam, dotting it evenly over the cake cubes.

3 Reserve a few raspberries for decoration. Make a layer of half of the remaining raspberries on top.

4 Pour over half of the custard, covering the fruit and cake. Repeat the layers. Cover and chill for at least 2 hours.

5 Before serving, spoon the sweetened whipped cream evenly over the top. To decorate, sprinkle with toasted flaked almonds and arrange the reserved raspberries and the mint leaves on the top.

VARIATION

Use other ripe summer fruit such as apricots, peaches, nectarines and strawberries in the trifle, with jam and liqueur to suit.

Ruby Fruit Salad

After a rich main course, this port-flavoured fruit salad is light and refreshing. Use any combination of fruit that is available.

INGREDIENTS

Serves 8

115g/4oz/8 tbsp caster sugar

1 cinnamon stick

4 cloves

pared rind of 1 orange

300ml/½ pint/1¼ cups port

2 oranges

1 small ripe Ogen, Charentais or
  honeydew melon

4 small bananas

2 dessert apples

225g/8oz seedless grapes

1 Put the sugar, spices, pared orange rind and 300ml/½ pint/1¼ cups of water into a pan and stir over a gentle heat to dissolve the sugar. Then bring to the boil, cover with a lid and simmer for 10 minutes. Leave to cool, then add the port.

2 Strain the liquid (to remove the spices and orange rind) into a bowl. With a sharp knife, cut off all the skin and pith from the oranges. Then, holding each orange over the bowl to catch the juice, cut away the segments, by slicing between the membrane that divides each segment and allowing the segments to drop into the syrup. Squeeze the remaining pith to release any juice.

3 Cut the melon in half, remove the seeds and scoop out the flesh with a melon baller, or cut it in small cubes. Add it to the syrup.

4 Peel the bananas and cut them diagonally in 1cm/½in slices. Quarter and core the apples and cut them in small cubes. Leave the skin on, or peel them if it is tough. Halve the grapes if large or leave them whole. Stir all the fruit into the syrup, cover with clear film and chill for 1 hour before serving.

Summer Pudding

Unbelievably simple to make and totally delicious, this is a real warm weather classic.

INGREDIENTS

Serves 4

about 8 thin slices day-old white bread, crusts removed

800g/1¾lb mixed summer fruits

about 30ml/2 tbsp granulated sugar

1 Cut a round from one slice of bread to fit in the base of a 1.2 litre/2 pint/5 cup pudding basin, then cut strips of bread about 5cm/2in wide to line the basin, overlapping the strips.

2 Gently heat the fruit, sugar and 30ml/2 tbsp water in a large heavy saucepan, shaking the pan occasionally, until the juices begin to run.

3 Reserve about 45ml/3 tbsp fruit juice, then spoon the fruit and remaining juice into the basin, taking care not to dislodge the bread lining.

4 Cut the remaining bread to fit entirely over the fruit. Stand the basin on a plate and cover with a saucer or small plate that will just fit inside the top of the basin. Place a heavy weight on top. Chill the pudding and the reserved fruit juice overnight.

5 Run a knife carefully around the inside of the basin rim, then invert the pudding on to a cold serving plate. Pour over the reserved juice and serve.

COOK'S TIP

Summer pudding freezes well so make an extra one to enjoy during the winter.

Apricot and Pear Filo Roulade

This is a very quick way of making a strudel – normally, very time consuming to do – it tastes delicious all the same!

INGREDIENTS

Serves 4–6

115g/4oz/½ cup ready-to-eat dried
   apricots, chopped
30ml/2 tbsp apricot jam
5ml/1 tsp lemon juice
50g/2oz/¼ cup soft brown sugar
2 medium pears, peeled, cored
   and chopped
50g/2oz/½ cup ground almonds
30ml/2 tbsp slivered almonds
25g/1oz/2 tbsp butter
8 sheets filo pastry
icing sugar, to dust

1 Put the apricots, apricot jam, lemon juice, brown sugar and pears into a pan and heat gently, stirring, for 5–7 minutes.

2 Remove from the heat and cool. Mix in the ground and slivered almonds. Preheat the oven to 200°C/400°F/Gas 6. Melt the butter in a pan.

3 Lightly grease a baking sheet. Layer the pastry on the baking sheet, brushing each layer with the melted butter.

4 Spoon the filling down the pastry just to one side of the centre and within 2.5cm/1in of each end. Lift the other side of the pastry up by sliding a palette knife underneath.

5 Fold this pastry over the filling, tucking the edge under. Seal the ends neatly and brush all over with butter again.

6 Bake for 15–20 minutes, until golden. Dust with icing sugar and serve hot.

Red Berry Tart with Lemon Cream Filling

This flan is best filled just before serving so the pastry remains mouth-wateringly crisp. Select red berry fruits such as strawberries, raspberries or redcurrants.

INGREDIENTS

Serves 6–8

150g/5oz/1¼ cups plain flour

25g/1oz/¼ cup cornflour

40g/1½oz/5 tbsp icing sugar

90g/3½oz/7 tbsp butter

5ml/1 tsp vanilla essence

2 egg yolks, beaten

sprig of mint, to decorate

For the filling

200g/7oz/scant 1 cup cream cheese

45ml/3 tbsp lemon curd

grated rind and juice of 1 lemon

icing sugar, to sweeten (optional)

225g/8oz/2 cups mixed red berry fruits

45ml/3 tbsp redcurrant jelly

1 Sift the flour, cornflour and icing sugar together, then rub in the butter until the mixture resembles breadcrumbs.

2 Beat the vanilla into the egg yolks, then mix into the crumbs to make a firm dough, adding cold water if necessary.

3 Roll out and line a 23cm/9in round flan tin, pressing the dough well up the sides. Prick the base with a fork and allow it to rest in the fridge for 30 minutes.

4 Preheat the oven to 200°C/400°F/Gas 6. Line the flan with greaseproof paper and baking beans. Place the tin on a baking sheet and bake for 20 minutes, removing the paper and beans for the last 5 minutes. When cooked, cool and remove the pastry case from the flan tin.

5 Cream the cheese, lemon curd and lemon rind and juice, adding icing sugar to sweeten, if you wish. Spread the mixture into the base of the flan.

6 Top the flan with the fruits. Gently warm the redcurrant jelly and trickle it over the fruits just before serving the flan decorated with a sprig of mint.

VARIATIONS

There are all sorts of delightful variations to this recipe. For instance, leave out the redcurrant jelly and sprinkle lightly with icing sugar or decorate with fresh strawberry leaves. Alternatively, top with sliced kiwi fruit or bananas slices sprinkled with lemon juice.

Chocolate Layer Cake

The cake layers can be made ahead, wrapped and frozen for future use. Always defrost cakes completely before icing.

Serves 10–12

unsweetened cocoa for dusting

225g/8oz can cooked whole beetroot, drained and juice reserved

115g/4oz/½ cup unsalted butter, softened

500g/1¼lb/2½ cups light brown sugar, firmly packed

3 eggs

15ml/1 tbsp vanilla essence

75g/3oz unsweetened chocolate, melted

275g/10oz/2¼ cups plain flour

10ml/2 tsp baking powder

2.5ml/½ tsp salt

120ml/4fl oz/½ cup buttermilk

chocolate curls (optional)

For the chocolate ganache frosting

475ml/16fl oz/2 cups whipping or double cream

500g/1¼lb fine quality, bittersweet or semi-sweet chocolate, chopped

15ml/1 tbsp vanilla essence

1 Preheat the oven to 180°C/ 350°F/ Gas 4. Grease two 23cm/9in cake tins and dust the bottoms and sides with cocoa. Grate the beetroot and add to the beet juice. With an electric mixer, beat the butter, brown sugar, eggs and vanilla until pale and fluffy (3–5 minutes). Reduce the speed and beat in the chocolate.

2 In a bowl, sift the flour, baking powder and salt. With the mixer on low speed, alternately beat in the flour mixture in fourths and buttermilk in thirds. Add the beets and juice and beat for 1 minute. Divide between the tins and bake for 30–35 minutes or until a cake tester inserted in the centre comes out clean. Cool for 10 minutes, unmould and cool.

3 To make the frosting, in a heavy-based saucepan over medium heat, heat the cream until it just begins to boil, stirring occasionally to prevent it from scorching.

4 Remove from the heat and stir in the chocolate, stirring constantly until melted and smooth. Stir in the vanilla. Strain into a bowl and refrigerate, stirring every 10 minutes, until spreadable, about 1 hour.

5 Assemble the cake. Place one layer on a serving plate and spread with one-third of the ganache. Turn the cake layer bottom side up, top with the second layer and spread the remaining ganache over the top and sides of the cake. If using, top with curls. Allow to set for 20–30 minutes, then refrigerate.

Marbled Swiss Roll

Simply sensational – that's the combination of light chocolate sponge and walnut chocolate buttercream.

INGREDIENTS

Serves 6–8

90g/3½oz/scant 1 cup plain flour
15ml/1 tbsp cocoa powder
25g/1oz plain chocolate, grated
25g/1oz white chocolate, grated
3 eggs
115g/4oz/generous ½ cup caster sugar

For the filling

75g/3oz/6 tbsp unsalted butter or
    margarine, softened
175g/6oz/1½ cups icing sugar
15ml/1 tbsp cocoa powder
2.5ml/½ tsp vanilla essence
45ml/3 tbsp chopped walnuts
plain and white chocolate curls, to
    decorate (optional)

1 Preheat the oven to 200°C/400°F/Gas 6. Grease a 30 x 20cm/12 x 8in Swiss roll tin and line with non-stick baking paper. Sift half the flour with the cocoa into a bowl. Stir in the grated plain chocolate. Sift the remaining flour into another bowl; stir in the grated white chocolate.

2 Whisk the eggs and sugar in a heatproof bowl; set over a saucepan of hot water until the mixture holds its shape when the whisk is lifted.

3 Remove the bowl from the heat and tip half the mixture into a separate bowl. Fold the white chocolate mixture into one portion, then fold the plain chocolate mixture into the other. Stir 15ml/1 tbsp boiling water into each half to soften the mixtures.

4 Place alternate spoonfuls of the mixture in the prepared tin and swirl lightly together for a marbled effect. Bake for about 12–15 minutes, or until firm. Turn out on to a sheet of non-stick baking paper.

5 Trim the edges to neaten and cover with a damp, clean dish towel. Cool.

6 For the filling, beat the butter or margarine, icing sugar, cocoa powder and vanilla essence together in a bowl until smooth, then mix in the walnuts.

7 Uncover the sponge, lift off the baking paper and spread the surface with the buttercream. Roll up carefully from a long side and place on a serving plate. Decorate with plain and white chocolate curls, if wished.

Angel Food Cake

This cake is beautifully light. The secret? Sifting the flour over and over again to let plenty of air into it.

Serves 12–14

115g/4oz/1 cup sifted cake flour
285g/10½oz/1½ cups caster sugar
300ml/½ pint/1¼ cups egg whites (about
   10–11 eggs)
6.5ml/1¼ tsp cream of tartar
1.5ml/¼ tsp salt
5ml/1 tsp vanilla essence
1.5ml/¼ tsp almond essence
icing sugar, for dusting

1 Preheat the oven to 160°C/ 325°F/Gas 3. Sift the flour before measuring, then sift it four times with 90g/3½oz/½ cup of the sugar. Transfer to a bowl.

2 With an electric mixer, beat the egg whites until foamy. Sift over the cream of tartar and salt and continue to beat until they hold soft peaks when the beaters are lifted.

3 Add the remaining sugar in three batches, beating well after each addition. Stir in the vanilla and almond essence.

4 Add the flour mixture, ½ cup at a time, and fold in gently with a large metal spoon after each addition.

5 Transfer to an ungreased 25cm/10in straight-sided ring mould and bake until delicately browned on top, about 1 hour.

6 Turn the ring mould upside down on to a cake rack and let cool for 1 hour. If the cake does not unmould, run a spatula around the edge to loosen it. Invert on to a serving plate.

7 When cool, lay a star-shaped template on top of the cake, sift with icing sugar, and lift off.

Chocolate and Cherry Polenta Cake

Polenta and almonds add an unusual nutty texture to this delicious dessert.

INGREDIENTS

Serves 8

50g/2oz/⅓ cup quick-cook polenta

200g/7oz plain chocolate, broken into squares

5 eggs, separated

175g/6oz/¾ cup caster sugar

115g/4oz/1 cup ground almonds

60ml/4 tbsp plain flour

finely grated rind of 1 orange

115g/4oz/½ cup glacé cherries, halved

icing sugar, for dusting

1 Place the polenta in a heatproof bowl and pour over just enough boiling water to cover, about 120ml/4fl oz/½ cup. Stir well, then cover the bowl and leave to stand for about 30 minutes, until the polenta has absorbed all the excess moisture.

2 Preheat the oven to 190°C/ 375°F/Gas 5. Grease a deep 22cm/8½in round cake tin and line the base with non-stick baking paper. Melt the chocolate in a heatproof bowl over hot water.

3 Whisk the egg yolks with the sugar in a bowl until thick and pale. Beat in the chocolate, then fold in the polenta, ground almonds, flour and orange rind.

4 Whisk the egg whites in a clean bowl until stiff. Stir 15ml/1 tbsp of the whites into the chocolate mixture, then fold in the rest. Finally, fold in the cherries.

5 Scrape the mixture into the prepared tin and bake for 45–55 minutes or until well risen and firm to the touch. Cool on a rack. Dust with icing sugar to serve.

Lemon Coconut Layer Cake

The flavours of lemon and coconut complement each other beautifully in this light dessert cake.

Serves 8–10

115g/4oz/1 cup plain flour
pinch of salt
8 eggs
350g/12oz/1¾ cups granulated sugar
15ml/1 tbsp grated orange rind
grated rind of 2 lemons
juice of 1 lemon
40g/1½oz/½ cup desiccated coconut
30ml/2 tbsp cornflour
75g/3oz/6 tbsp butter

For the frosting

115g/4oz/½ cup unsalted butter, at room
    temperature
115g/4oz/1 cup icing sugar
grated rind of 1 lemon
90–120ml/6–8 tbsp fresh lemon juice
400g/14oz desiccated coconut

1 Preheat the oven to 180°C/ 350°F/Gas 4. Line three 20cm/8in cake tins with baking parchment and grease. In a bowl, sift together the flour and salt and set aside.

2 Place six of the eggs in a large heatproof bowl set over hot water. With an electric mixer, beat until frothy. Gradually beat in 150g/5oz/¾ cup of the granulated sugar until the mixture doubles in volume and is thick enough to leave a ribbon trail when the beaters are lifted, which takes about 10 minutes.

3 Remove the bowl from the hot water. Fold in the orange rind, half the grated lemon rind and 15ml/1 tbsp of the lemon juice until blended. Fold in the coconut.

4 Sift over the flour mixture in three batches, folding in thoroughly after each addition.

5 Divide the mixture between the prepared tins.

6 Bake until the cakes pull away from the sides of the tin, 25–30 minutes. Let stand 3–5 minutes, then unmould and transfer to a cooling rack.

7 In a bowl, blend the cornflour with a little cold water to dissolve. Whisk in the remaining eggs until just blended. Set aside.

8 In a saucepan, combine the remaining lemon rind and juice, the remaining sugar, butter and 250ml/8fl oz/1 cup of water.

9 Over a moderate heat, bring the mixture to the boil. Whisk in the eggs and cornflour, and return to the boil. Whisk continuously until thick, about 5 minutes. Remove from the heat. Cover with baking parchment to stop a skin forming and set aside.

10 For the frosting, cream the butter and icing sugar until smooth. Stir in the lemon rind and enough lemon juice to obtain a thick, spreadable consistency.

11 Sandwich the three cake layers with the lemon custard mixture. Spread the frosting over the top and sides. Cover the cake with the coconut, pressing it in gently.

Carrot Cake with Maple Butter Frosting

A good, quick dessert cake for a family supper.

Serves 12

450g/1lb carrots, peeled
175g/6oz/1½ cups plain flour
10ml/2 tsp baking powder
2.5ml/½ tsp baking soda
5ml/1 tsp salt
10ml/2 tsp ground cinnamon
4 eggs
10ml/2 tsp vanilla essence
225g/8oz/1 cup dark brown sugar,
    firmly packed
90g/3½oz/½ cup granulated sugar
300ml/½ pint/1¼ cups sunflower oil
115g/4oz/1 cup walnuts, finely chopped
65g/2½oz/½ cup raisins
walnut halves, to decorate (optional)

For the frosting
75g/3oz/6 tbsp unsalted butter, at room
    temperature
375g/12oz/3 cups icing sugar
50ml/2fl oz/¼ cup maple syrup

1 Preheat the oven to 180°C/
350°F/Gas 4. Line a 28 x 20cm/
11 x 8in rectangular cake tin with
non-stick baking paper and grease.
Grate the carrots and set aside.

2 Sift the flour, baking powder,
baking soda, salt and
cinnamon into a bowl. Set aside.

3 With an electric mixer, beat the
eggs until blended. Add the
vanilla, sugars and oil; beat to
incorporate. Add the dry
ingredients, in three batches,
folding in well after each addition.

4 Add the carrots, walnuts and
raisins and fold in thoroughly.

5 Pour the batter into the
prepared tin and bake until the
cake springs back when touched
lightly, 40–45 minutes. Let stand
10 minutes, then unmould and
transfer to a rack.

6 For the frosting, cream the
butter with half the sugar until
soft. Add the syrup, then beat in
the remaining sugar until blended.

7 Spread the frosting over the
top of the cake. Using a metal
spatula, make decorative ridges.
Cut into squares. Decorate with
walnut halves, if liked.

Black and White Pound Cake

A good cake for packed lunches and picnics as it cuts into neat slices with no messy filling, or serve with custard for dessert.

INGREDIENTS

Serves 16

115g/4oz plain chocolate, broken into squares

350g/12oz/3 cups plain flour

5ml/1 tsp baking powder

450g/1lb/2 cups butter, at room temperature

650g/1lb 7oz/3 cups sugar

15ml/1 tbsp vanilla essence

10 eggs, at room temperature

icing sugar, for dusting

1 Preheat the oven to 180°C/ 350°F/Gas 4. Line the bottom of a 25cm/10in straight-sided ring mould with non-stick baking paper and grease. Dust with flour spread evenly with a brush.

2 Melt the chocolate in the top of a double boiler, or in a heatproof bowl set over a pan of hot water. Stir occasionally. Set aside.

3 In a bowl, sift together the flour and baking powder. In another bowl, cream the butter, sugar and vanilla essence with an electric mixer until light and fluffy. Add the eggs, two at a time, then gradually incorporate the flour mixture on low speed.

4 Spoon half of the batter into the prepared mould.

COOK'S TIP

This is also known as Marbled Cake because of its distinctive appearance.

5 Stir the chocolate into the remaining batter, then spoon into the mould. With a metal spatula, swirl the two batters to create a marbled effect.

6 Bake until a cake tester inserted in the centre comes out clean, about 1¼ hours. Cover with foil halfway through baking. Let stand 15 minutes, then unmould and transfer to a cooling rack. To serve, dust with icing sugar.

Chocolate Mousse Strawberry Layer Cake

The strawberries used in this cake can be replaced by raspberries or blackberries and the appropriate flavour liqueur.

INGREDIENTS

Serves 10

115g/4oz fine quality white chocolate, chopped

120ml/4fl oz/½ cup whipping or double cream

120ml/4fl oz/½ cup milk

15ml/1 tbsp rum or vanilla essence

115g/4oz/½ cup unsalted butter, softened

175g/6oz/generous ¾ cup granulated sugar

3 eggs

275g/10oz/2½ cups plain flour

5ml/1 tsp baking powder

pinch of salt

675g/1½lb fresh strawberries, sliced, plus extra for decoration

750ml/1¼ pints/3 cups whipping cream

30ml/2 tbsp rum or strawberry-flavoured liqueur

For the white chocolate mousse

250g/9oz fine quality white chocolate, chopped

350ml/12fl oz/1½ cups whipping or double cream

30ml/2 tbsp rum or strawberry-flavoured liqueur

1 Preheat the oven to 180°C/350°F/ Gas 4. Grease and flour two 23 x 5cm/9 x 2in cake tins. Line the base of the tins with non-stick baking paper. Melt the chocolate and cream in a double boiler over a low heat, stirring until smooth. Stir in the milk and rum or vanilla essence; set aside to cool.

2 In a large bowl with an electric mixer, beat the butter and sugar until light and creamy. Add the eggs one at a time, beating well.

3 In a small bowl, stir together the flour, baking powder and salt. Alternately add flour and melted chocolate to the eggs in batches, until just blended. Pour the batter evenly into the tins.

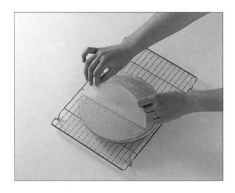

4 Bake for 20–25 minutes until a cake tester inserted in the centre comes out clean. Cool on a wire rack for 10 minutes. Turn the cakes out on to a wire rack, peel off the paper and cool completely.

5 Prepare the mousse. In a medium saucepan over low heat, melt the chocolate and cream until smooth, stirring frequently. Stir in the rum or strawberry-flavoured liqueur and pour into a bowl. Chill until just set. With a whisk, whip until the mixture has a "mousse" consistency.

6 Slice both cake layers in half crossways. Sandwich the four layers together with the mousse and strawberries.

7 Whip the cream with the rum or liqueur until firm peaks form. Spread half over the top and sides of the cake. Spoon the remaining cream into an icing bag with a star tip and pipe scrolls on the top. Garnish with the remaining strawberries.

Death by Chocolate

One of the richest chocolate cakes ever, so serve in thin slices.

INGREDIENTS

Serves 16–20

225g/8oz plain dark chocolate, broken
    into squares
115g/4oz/½ cup unsalted butter
150ml/¼ pint/⅔ cup milk
225g/8oz/1¼ cups light muscovado sugar
10ml/2 tsp vanilla essence
2 eggs, separated
150ml/¼ pint/⅔ cup soured cream
225g/8oz/2 cups self-raising flour
5ml/1 tsp baking powder

For the filling
60ml/4 tbsp seedless raspberry jam
60ml/4 tbsp brandy
400g/14oz plain dark chocolate, broken
    into squares
200g/7oz/scant 1 cup unsalted butter

For the topping
250ml/8fl oz/1 cup double cream
225g/8oz plain dark chocolate, broken
    into squares
plain and white chocolate curls,
    to decorate
chocolate-dipped physalis (Cape
    gooseberries), to serve (optional)

1 Preheat the oven to 180°C/350°F/ Gas 4. Grease and base-line a deep 23cm/9in springform cake tin. Place the chocolate, butter and milk in a saucepan. Heat gently until smooth. Remove from the heat, beat in sugar and vanilla, then cool.

2 Beat the egg yolks and cream in a bowl, then beat into the chocolate mixture. Sift the flour and baking powder over the surface and fold in. Whisk the egg whites in a grease-free bowl until stiff; fold into the mixture.

3 Scrape into the prepared tin and bake for 45–55 minutes, or until firm to the touch. Cool in the tin for 15 minutes, then invert to a wire rack to cool.

4 Slice the cold cake horizontally to make three even layers. In a small saucepan, warm the jam with 15ml/1 tbsp of the brandy, then brush over two of the layers. Heat the remaining brandy in a saucepan with the chocolate and butter, stirring, until smooth. Cool until beginning to thicken.

5 Spread the bottom layer of the cake with half the chocolate filling, taking care not to disturb the jam. Top with a second layer, jam side up, and spread with the remaining filling. Top with the final layer and press lightly. Leave to set.

6 To make the topping, heat the cream and chocolate together in a saucepan over a low heat, stirring frequently until the chocolate has melted. Pour into a bowl, leave to cool, then whisk until the mixture begins to hold its shape.

7 Spread the top and sides of the cake with the chocolate ganache. Decorate with chocolate curls and, if liked, chocolate-dipped physalis (Cape gooseberries).

Simple Chocolate Cake

An easy, everyday chocolate cake which can be filled with butter-cream, or with a rich chocolate ganache for a special occasion.

INGREDIENTS

Serves 6–8

115g/4oz plain chocolate, broken into
    squares
45ml/3 tbsp milk
150g/5oz/⅔ cup unsalted butter or
    margarine, softened
150g/5oz/scant 1 cup light muscovado
    sugar
3 eggs
200g/7oz/1¾ cups self-raising flour
15ml/1 tbsp cocoa powder

For the buttercream
75g/3oz/6 tbsp unsalted butter or
    margarine, softened
175g/6oz/1½ cups icing sugar
15ml/1 tbsp cocoa powder
2.5ml/½ tsp vanilla essence
icing sugar and cocoa powder, for dusting

1 Preheat the oven to 180°C/
350°F/Gas 4. Grease two
18cm/7in round sandwich cake
tins and line the base of each with
non-stick baking paper. Melt the
chocolate with the milk in a
heatproof bowl set over a pan of
simmering water.

2 Cream the butter or
margarine with the sugar in a
mixing bowl until pale and fluffy.
Add the eggs one at a time, beating
well after each addition. Stir in the
chocolate mixture until it is
well combined.

3 Sift the flour and cocoa over
the mixture and fold in with
a metal spoon until evenly mixed.
Scrape into the prepared tins,
smooth level and bake for
35–40 minutes or until well risen
and firm. Turn out on wire racks
and leave to cool.

4 To make the buttercream, beat
the butter or margarine, icing
sugar, cocoa powder and vanilla
essence together in a bowl until the
mixture is smooth.

5 Sandwich the cake layers
together with the buttercream.
Dust with a mixture of icing sugar
and cocoa just before serving.

Pineapple Upside-Down Cake

This is a perennial favourite to serve in winter or summer.

INGREDIENTS

Serves 8

115g/4oz/½ cup butter

225g/8oz/1 cup dark brown sugar, firmly packed

450g/16oz can pineapple slices, drained

4 eggs, separated

grated rind of 1 lemon

pinch of salt

90g/3½oz/½ cup granulated sugar

85g/3¼oz/¾ cup plain flour

5ml/1 tsp baking powder

1 Preheat the oven to 180°C/350°F/Gas 4. Melt the butter in an ovenproof cast-iron frying pan, about 25cm/10in in diameter. Remove 15ml/1 tbsp of the melted butter and set aside.

2 Add the brown sugar to the frying pan and stir until blended. Place the drained pineapple slices on top in one layer. Set aside.

3 In a bowl, whisk together the egg yolks, reserved butter and lemon rind until smooth and well blended. Set aside.

4 With an electric mixer, beat the egg whites with the salt until stiff. Fold in the granulated sugar, 30ml/2 tbsp at a time. Fold in the egg yolk mixture.

5 Sift the flour and baking powder together. Fold into the egg mixture in three batches.

6 Pour the batter over the pineapple and smooth level.

7 Bake until a cake tester inserted in the centre comes out clean, about 30 minutes.

8 While still hot, place a serving plate on top of the frying pan, bottom side up. Holding them together with oven gloves, flip over. Serve hot or cold.

Peach and Blueberry Pie

The unusual combination of fruits in this pie looks especially good with a lattice pastry topping.

INGREDIENTS

Serves 8

225g/8oz/2 cups plain flour
pinch of salt
10ml/2 tsp sugar
150g/5oz/10 tbsp cold butter or margarine
1 egg yolk
30ml/2 tbsp milk, to glaze

For the filling

450g/1lb fresh peaches, peeled, stoned
  and sliced
275g/10oz/2 cups fresh blueberries
150g/5oz/¾ cup caster sugar
30ml/2 tbsp fresh lemon juice
40g/1½oz/⅓ cup plain flour
large pinch of grated nutmeg
25g/1oz/2 tbsp butter or margarine, cut
  into tiny pieces

1 To make the pastry, sift the flour, salt and sugar into a bowl. Rub the butter or margarine into the dry ingredients as quickly as possible until the mixture resembles coarse breadcrumbs.

2 Mix the egg yolk with 50ml/ 2fl oz/¼ cup of iced water and sprinkle over the flour mixture. Combine with a fork until the dough holds together. If the dough is too crumbly, add a little more water, 15ml/1 tbsp at a time. Gather the dough into a ball and flatten into a round. Place in a sealed polythene bag and chill for at least 20 minutes.

3 Roll out two-thirds of the pastry between two sheets of greaseproof paper to a thickness of about 3mm/⅛in. Use to line a 23cm/9in pie dish.

4 Trim the pastry all around, leaving a 1cm/½in overhang. Fold the overhang under to form the edge. Using a fork, press the edge to the rim of the pie dish.

5 Gather the trimmings and remaining pastry into a ball, and roll out to a thickness of about 5mm/¼in. Using a pastry wheel or sharp knife, cut into long, 1cm/½in wide strips. Chill both the pastry case and the strips of pastry for 20 minutes. Meanwhile, preheat the oven to 200°C/400°F/Gas 6.

6 Line the pastry case with greaseproof paper and fill with dried beans. Bake for 7–10 minutes, until the pastry is just set. Remove from the oven and carefully lift out the paper with the beans. Prick the base of the pastry case with a fork, then return to the oven and bake for a further 5 minutes. Leave to cool slightly before filling. Leave the oven on.

7 For the filling, place the peach slices and blueberries in a bowl and stir in the sugar, lemon juice, flour and nutmeg. Spoon the fruit mixture into the pastry case. Dot the top with the pieces of butter or margarine.

8 Weave a lattice top with the chilled pastry strips, pressing the ends to the edge of the baked pastry case. Brush the strips with the milk.

9 Bake the pie for 15 minutes. Reduce the oven temperature to 180°C/350°F/Gas 4, and continue baking for another 30 minutes, until the filling is tender and bubbling and the pastry lattice is golden. If the pastry becomes too brown, cover loosely with a piece of foil. Serve the pie warm or at room temperature.

COOK'S TIP

Don't over-chill the pastry strips. If they become too firm, they may crack and break as you weave them into a lattice.

Rhubarb Pie

Use a biscuit cutter to cut out decorative pastry shapes and make this pie extra special.

Serves 6

175g/6oz/1½ cups plain flour
2.5ml/½ tsp salt
10ml/2 tsp caster sugar
75g/3oz/6 tbsp cold butter or margarine
30ml/2 tbsp single cream
single or double cream, to serve

For the filling

1kg/2¼lb fresh rhubarb, cut into
    2.5cm/1in slices
30ml/2 tbsp cornflour
1 egg
275g/10oz/1½ cups caster sugar
15ml/1 tbsp grated orange rind

1 To make the pastry, sift the flour, salt and sugar into a bowl. Using a pastry blender or two knives, cut the butter or margarine into the dry ingredients as quickly as possible until the mixture resembles breadcrumbs.

2 Sprinkle the flour mixture with about 50ml/2fl oz/¼ cup of iced water and mix until the dough just holds together. If the dough is too crumbly, add a little more water, 15ml/1 tbsp at a time.

3 Gather the dough into a ball, flatten into a round, place in a polythene bag and put in the fridge for 20 minutes.

4 Roll out the pastry between two sheets of greaseproof paper to a 3mm/⅛in thickness. Use to line a 23cm/9in pie dish or tin. Trim all around, leaving a 1cm/½in overhang. Fold the overhang under the edge and flute. Chill the case and trimmings for 30 minutes.

5 To make the filling, put the rhubarb in a bowl, sprinkle with the cornflour and toss to coat.

6 Preheat the oven to 220°C/ 425°F/Gas 7. Beat the egg with the sugar in a bowl until thoroughly blended, then mix in the orange rind.

7 Stir the sugar mixture into the rhubarb and mix well together, then spoon the fruit into the prepared pastry case.

8 Roll out the pastry trimmings. Stamp out decorative shapes with a biscuit cutter.

9 Arrange the pastry shapes on top of the pie. Brush the shapes and the edge of the pastry case with cream.

10 Bake the pie for 30 minutes. Reduce the oven temperature to 160°C/325°F/Gas 3 and continue baking for a further 15–20 minutes, until the pastry is golden brown and the rhubarb is tender. Serve the pie hot with cream.

Chocolate Pecan Torte

This torte uses finely ground nuts instead of flour. Toast then cool the nuts before grinding finely in a blender or food processor. Do not over-grind the nuts, as the oils will form a paste.

Serves 16

200g/7oz bittersweet or plain chocolate, chopped

150g/5oz/10 tbsp unsalted butter, cut into pieces

4 eggs

90g/3½oz/½ cup caster sugar

10ml/2 tsp vanilla essence

115g/4oz/1 cup ground pecans

10ml/2 tsp ground cinnamon

24 toasted pecan halves, to decorate (optional)

For the chocolate honey glaze

115g/4oz bittersweet or semi-sweet chocolate, chopped

50g/2oz/¼ cup unsalted butter, cut into pieces

30ml/2 tbsp clear honey

pinch of ground cinnamon

1 Preheat the oven to 180°C/ 350°F/Gas 4. Grease a 20 x 5cm/8 x 2in springform tin; line with baking paper then grease the paper. Wrap the bottom and sides of the tin with foil to prevent water seeping in. In a saucepan over a low heat, melt the chocolate and butter, stirring until smooth. Remove from the heat. In a mixing bowl with an electric mixer, beat the eggs, sugar and vanilla essence until frothy, 1–2 minutes. Stir in the melted chocolate, ground nuts and cinnamon. Pour into the prepared tin.

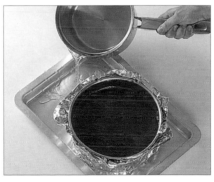

2 Place the foil-wrapped tin in a large roasting tin and pour boiling water into the roasting tin, to come 2cm/¾in up the side of the springform tin. Bake for 25–30 minutes until the edge of the cake is set, but the centre is soft. Remove the tin from the water bath and remove the foil. Cool on a rack.

3 Prepare the glaze. In a small saucepan over low heat, melt the chocolate, butter, honey and cinnamon, stirring until smooth; remove from the heat. Carefully dip the toasted pecan halves halfway into the glaze and place on a non-stick baking paper-lined baking sheet until it is set.

4 Remove the sides from the tin and invert the cake on to a wire rack. Remove the tin bottom and paper, so the bottom of the cake is now the top. Pour the thickened glaze over the cake, tilting the rack slightly to spread the glaze. Use a metal palette knife to smooth the sides. Arrange the glazed nuts around outside edge of the torte and allow the glaze to set.

Key Lime Pie

Key limes come from Florida but if they are not available, ordinary limes will do just as well.

INGREDIENTS

Serves 8

3 large egg yolks

400g/14oz can sweetened condensed milk

15ml/1 tbsp grated Key lime rind

120ml/4fl oz/½ cup fresh Key lime juice

green food colouring (optional)

120ml/4fl oz/½ cup whipping cream

For the crust

1¼ cups digestive biscuit crumbs

75ml/5 tbsp butter or margarine, melted

1 Preheat the oven to 180°C/350°F/Gas 4. For the crust, place the biscuit crumbs in a bowl and add the butter or margarine. Mix to combine.

2 Press the crumbs evenly over the bottom and sides of a 23cm/9in pie dish or tin. Bake for 8 minutes. Let cool.

3 Beat the yolks until thick. Beat in the milk, lime rind and juice, and colouring, if using. Pour into the prebaked pie crust and refrigerate until set, about 4 hours. To serve, whip the cream. Pipe a lattice pattern on top, or spoon dollops around the edge.

Fruit Tartlets

The chocolate pastry cases make a dramatic base to these tartlets.

INGREDIENTS

Makes 8

215g/7½oz/¾ cup redcurrant or grape jelly

15ml/1 tbsp fresh lemon juice

175ml/6fl oz/¾ cup whipping cream

675g/1½lb fresh fruit, such as strawberries, raspberries, kiwi fruit, peaches, grapes or blueberries, peeled and sliced as necessary

For the pastry

150g/5oz/⅔ cup cold butter, cut in pieces

65g/2½oz/⅓ cup dark brown sugar, firmly packed

45ml/3 tbsp unsweetened cocoa powder

175g/6oz/1½ cups plain flour

1 egg white

1 For the pastry, combine the butter, brown sugar and cocoa over low heat. When the butter is melted, remove from the heat and sift over the flour. Stir, then add just enough egg white to bind the mixture. Gather into a ball, wrap in greaseproof paper, and chill for at least 30 minutes.

2 Preheat the oven to 180°C/350°F/Gas 4. Grease eight 7.5cm/3in tartlet tins. Roll out the dough between two sheets of greaseproof paper and stamp out eight 10cm/4in rounds with a fluted cutter.

3 Line the tartlet tins with dough. Prick the bottoms. Chill for 15 minutes.

4 Bake until firm, 20–25 minutes. Leave to cool, then remove from the tins.

5 Melt the jelly with the lemon juice. Brush a thin layer in the bottom of the tartlets. Whip the cream and spread a thin layer in the tartlet shells. Arrange the fruit on top. Brush evenly with the glaze and serve.

Cherry Pie

The woven lattice is the perfect finishing touch, although you can cheat and use a lattice pastry roller if you prefer.

INGREDIENTS

Serves 8

900g/2lb fresh Morello cherries, stoned, or
   2 x 450g /1lb cans or jars, drained and
   stoned
65g/2½oz/generous ¾ cup caster sugar
25g/1oz/¼ cup plain flour
25ml/1½ tbsp fresh lemon juice
1.5ml/¼ tsp almond essence
25g/1oz/2 tbsp butter or margarine

For the pastry
225g/8oz/2 cups plain flour
5ml/1 tsp salt
175g/6oz/¾ cup lard or vegetable fat

1 For the pastry, sift the flour and salt into a mixing bowl. Using a pastry blender, cut in the fat until the mixture resembles coarse breadcrumbs.

2 Sprinkle in 60–75ml/4–5 tbsp iced water, a tablespoon at a time, tossing lightly with your fingertips or a fork until the pastry forms a ball.

3 Preheat the oven to 220°C/ 425°F/Gas 7. Divide the pastry in half and shape each half into a ball. On a lightly floured surface, roll out one of the balls to a circle about 30cm/12in in diameter.

4 Use it to line a 23cm/9in pie tin, easing the pastry in and being careful not to stretch it. With scissors, trim off excess pastry, leaving a 1cm/½in overhang around the pie tin.

5 Roll out the remaining pastry to 3mm/⅛in thick. Cut out eleven strips 1cm/½in wide.

6 In a mixing bowl, combine the cherries, sugar, flour, lemon juice and almond essence. Spoon the mixture into the pastry case and dot the top with the butter or margarine.

7 To make the lattice, place five of the pastry strips evenly across the filling. Fold every other strip back. Lay the first strip across in the opposite direction. Continue in this pattern, folding back every other strip each time you add a cross strip.

8 Trim the ends of the lattice strips even with the case overhang. Press together so that the edge rests on the pie-tin rim. With your thumbs, flute the edge. Chill for 15 minutes.

9 Bake the pie for 30 minutes, covering the edge of the pastry case with foil, if necessary, to prevent over-browning. Let cool, in the tin, on a wire rack.

Mince Pies with Orange Cinnamon Pastry

Home-made mince pies are so much nicer than shop bought, especially with this tasty pastry.

INGREDIENTS

Makes 18

225g/8oz/2 cups plain flour
40g/1½oz icing sugar
10ml/2 tsp ground cinnamon
150g/5oz/10 tbsp butter
grated rind of 1 orange
225g/8oz/⅔ cup mincemeat
1 beaten egg, to glaze
icing sugar, to dust

1 Sift together the flour, icing sugar and cinnamon then rub in the butter until it forms crumbs. (This can be done in a food processor.) Stir in the grated orange rind.

2 Mix to a firm dough with about 60ml/4 tbsp ice cold water. Knead lightly, then roll out to a 5mm/¼in thickness.

3 Using a 6cm/2½in round cutter, cut out 18 circles, re-rolling as necessary. Then cut out 18 smaller 5cm/2in circles.

4 Line two bun tins with the 18 larger circles – they will fill one and a half tins. Spoon a small spoonful of mincemeat into each pastry case and top with the smaller pastry circles, pressing the edges lightly together to seal.

5 Glaze the tops of the pies with egg and leave to rest in the fridge for 30 minutes. Preheat the oven to 200°C/400°F/Gas 6.

6 Bake the pies for 15–20 minutes until they are golden brown. Remove them to wire racks to cool. Serve just warm and dusted with icing sugar.

Apple-Cranberry Lattice Pie

Use fresh or frozen cranberries for this classic American pie.

INGREDIENTS

Serves 8

grated rind of 1 orange

45ml/3 tbsp fresh orange juice

2 large, tart cooking apples

115g/4oz/1 cup cranberries

65g/2½oz/½ cup raisins

25g/1oz/¼ cup walnuts, chopped

225g/8oz/1 cup granulated sugar

115g/4oz/½ cup dark brown sugar

15ml/1 tbsp quick-cooking tapioca

For the pastry

225g/8oz/2 cups plain flour

2.5ml/½ tsp salt

90ml/6 tbsp cold butter, cut in pieces

60ml/4 tbsp cold lard, cut in pieces

15ml/1 tbsp granulated sugar,
  for sprinkling

1 For the pastry, sift the flour and salt into a bowl. Add the butter and lard and rub in until the mixture resembles coarse crumbs. With a fork, stir in just enough iced water to bind the dough. Gather into two equal balls, wrap in greaseproof paper, and chill for at least 20 minutes.

2 Put the orange rind and juice into a mixing bowl. Peel and core the apples and grate them into the bowl. Stir in the cranberries, raisins, walnuts, granulated sugar, brown sugar and tapioca.

3 Place a baking sheet in the oven and preheat to 200°C/400°F/Gas 6.

4 On a lightly floured surface, roll out one ball of dough about 3mm/⅛in thick. Transfer to a 23cm/9in pie tin and trim the edge. Spoon the cranberry and apple mixture into the shell.

5 Roll out the remaining dough to a circle about 28cm/11in in diameter. With a serrated pastry wheel, cut the dough into ten strips, 2cm/¾in wide. Place five strips horizontally across the top of the tart at 1-inch intervals. Weave in six vertical strips. Trim the edges. Sprinkle the top with 15ml/1 tbsp of sugar.

6 Bake for 20 minutes. Reduce the heat to 180°C/350°F/Gas 4 and bake until the crust is golden and the filling is bubbling, about 15 minutes more.

Lemon Meringue Pie

Serve this exactly as it is, hot, warm or cold. It doesn't need any accompaniment.

Serves 8

grated rind and juice of 1 large lemon

200g/7oz/1 cup caster sugar

25g/1oz/2 tbsp butter

45ml/3 tbsp cornflour

3 eggs, separated

pinch of salt

0.75ml/⅛ tsp cream of tartar

For the pastry

115g/4oz/1 cup plain flour

2.5ml/½ tsp salt

65g/2½oz/⅓ cup cold lard, cut into pieces

1 For the pastry, sift the flour and salt into a bowl. Add the lard and cut in with a pastry blender until the mixture resembles coarse crumbs. With a fork, stir in just enough iced water to bind the dough (about 30ml/ 2 tbsp). Gather the dough into a ball.

2 On a lightly floured surface, roll out the dough to 3mm/⅛in thick. Transfer to a 23cm/9in pie tin and trim the edge to leave a 1cm/½in overhang.

3 Fold the overhang under and crimp the edge. Chill the pie shell in the fridge for at least 20 minutes. Preheat the oven to 200°C/400°F/Gas 6.

4 Prick the dough all over with a fork. Line with greaseproof paper and fill with baking beans. Bake for 12 minutes. Remove the paper and beans and continue baking until golden, about 6–8 minutes more.

5 In a saucepan, combine the lemon rind and juice, 90g/ 3½oz/½ cup sugar, butter and 250ml/8fl oz/1 cup of water. Bring the mixture to the boil.

6 Meanwhile, in a mixing bowl, dissolve the cornflour in 15ml/1 tbsp cold water. Add the egg yolks.

7 Add the egg yolks to the lemon mixture and return to the boil, whisking continuously until the mixture thickens, about 5 minutes.

8 Cover the surface with grease-proof paper to prevent a skin forming and let cool.

9 For the meringue, using an electric mixer beat the egg whites with the salt and cream of tartar until they hold stiff peaks. Add the remaining sugar and beat until glossy.

10 Spoon the lemon mixture into the pie shell and spread level. Spoon the meringue on top, smoothing it up to the edge of the crust to seal. Bake until golden, 12–15 minutes.

Chocolate Chiffon Pie

This light and creamy dessert is as luxurious as its name suggests.

INGREDIENTS

Serves 8

175g/6oz plain chocolate squares

25g/1oz square bitter chocolate

250ml/8fl oz/1 cup milk

15ml/1 tbsp gelatine, or alternative

130g/4½oz/⅔ cup granulated sugar

2 large eggs, separated

5ml/1 tsp vanilla essence

350ml/12fl oz/1½ cups whipping cream

pinch of salt

whipped cream and chocolate curls, to decorate

For the crust

75g/3oz/1½ cups digestive biscuit crumbs

75g/3oz/6 tbsp butter, melted

1 Place a baking sheet in the oven and preheat to 180°C/350°F/Gas 4. For the crust, mix the digestive biscuit crumbs and butter in a bowl. Press the crumbs evenly over the bottom and sides of a 23cm/9in pie tin. Bake for 8 minutes. Let cool.

2 Chop the chocolate, then grind in a food processor or blender. Set aside.

3 Place the milk in the top of a double boiler or in a heatproof bowl. Sprinkle over the gelatine. Let stand 5 minutes to soften.

4 Set the top of the double boiler or heatproof bowl over hot water. Add 50g/2oz/⅓ cup of the sugar, the chocolate and egg yolks. Stir until dissolved. Add the vanilla essence.

5 Set the top of the double boiler in a bowl of ice and stir until the mixture reaches room temperature. Remove from the ice and set aside.

6 Whip the cream lightly. Set aside. With an electric mixer, beat the egg whites and salt until they hold soft peaks. Add the remaining sugar and beat only enough to blend.

7 Fold a dollop of egg whites into the chocolate mixture, then pour back into the whites and gently fold in.

8 Fold in the whipped cream and pour into the pastry shell. Put in the freezer until just set, about 5 minutes. If the centre sinks, fill with any remaining mixture. Chill for 3–4 hours. Decorate with whipped cream and chocolate curls. Serve cold.

Coconut Cream Pie

Once you have made the pastry, the delicious filling can be put together in moments.

INGREDIENTS

Serves 8

200g/7oz/2½ cups shredded coconut
115g/4oz/⅔ cup caster sugar
60ml/4 tbsp cornflour
pinch of salt
600ml/1 pint/2½ cups milk
50ml/2fl oz/¼ cup whipping cream
2 egg yolks
25g/1oz/2 tbsp unsalted butter
10ml/2 tsp vanilla essence

For the pastry

115g/4oz/1 cup plain flour
1.5ml/¼ tsp salt
40g/1½oz/3 tbsp cold butter, cut in pieces
25g/1oz/2 tbsp cold lard

1 For the pastry, sift the flour and salt into a bowl. Add the butter and lard and cut in with a pastry blender or two knives until the mixture resembles coarse breadcrumbs.

2 With a fork, stir in just enough iced water to bind the dough (30–45ml/2–3 tbsp). Gather into a ball, wrap in greaseproof paper and chill for at least 20 minutes.

3 Preheat the oven to 220°C/ 425°F/Gas 7. Roll out the dough 3mm/⅛in thick. Transfer to a 23cm/9in flan tin. Trim and flute the edges. Prick the bottom. Line with greaseproof paper and fill with baking beans. Bake for 10–12 minutes. Remove the paper and beans, reduce the heat to 180°C/350°F/Gas 4 and bake until brown, about 10–15 minutes more.

4 Spread 75g/3oz/1 cup of the coconut on a baking sheet and toast in the oven until golden, 6–8 minutes, stirring often. Set aside for decorating.

5 Put the sugar, cornflour and salt in a saucepan. In a bowl, whisk together the milk, cream and egg yolks. Add the egg mixture to the saucepan.

6 Cook over low heat, stirring constantly, until the mixture comes to the boil. Boil for 1 minute, then remove from the heat. Add the butter, vanilla essence and remaining coconut.

7 Pour into the pre-baked pastry case. When the filling is cool, sprinkle toasted coconut in a ring in the centre.

Peach Tart with Almond Cream

The almond cream filling should be baked until it is just turning brown. Take care not to overbake it or the delicate flavours will be spoilt.

INGREDIENTS

Serves 8–10

4 large ripe peaches

115g/4oz/⅔ cup blanched almonds

30ml/2 tbsp plain flour

90g/3½oz/7 tbsp unsalted butter, at room temperature

130g/4½oz/scant ¾ cup granulated sugar

1 egg

1 egg yolk

2.5ml/½ tsp vanilla essence, or 10ml/ 2 tsp rum

For the pastry

150g/5oz/1¼ cups flour

4ml/¾ tsp salt

90g/3½oz/7 tbsp cold unsalted butter, cut in pieces

1 egg yolk

1 For the pastry, sift the flour and salt into a bowl.

2 Add the butter and cut in with a pastry blender until the mixture resembles coarse crumbs. With a fork, stir in the egg yolk and just enough iced water (30–45ml/ 2–3 tbsp) to bind the dough. Gather into a ball, wrap in grease-proof paper and chill for at least 20 minutes. Place a baking sheet in the oven and preheat to 200°C/400°F/Gas 6.

3 On a lightly floured surface, roll out the pastry 3mm/⅛in thick. Transfer to a 25cm/10in flan tin. Trim the edge, prick the bottom and chill.

4 Score the bottoms of the peaches. Drop the peaches, one at a time, into boiling water. Leave for 20 seconds, then dip in cold water. Peel off the skins using a sharp knife.

5 Grind the almonds finely with the flour in a food processor, blender or nut grinder. With an electric mixer, cream the butter and 90g/3½oz/½ cup of the sugar until light and fluffy. Gradually beat in the egg and yolk. Stir in the almonds and vanilla or rum. Spread in the pastry shell.

6 Halve the peaches and remove the stones. Cut crosswise in thin slices and arrange on top of the almond cream like the spokes of a wheel; keep the slices of each peach-half together. Fan them out by pressing down gently at a slight angle.

7 Bake until the pastry begins to brown, 10–15 minutes. Lower the heat to 180°C/350°F/Gas 4 and continue baking until the almond cream sets, about 15 minutes more. Ten minutes before the end of the cooking time, sprinkle with the remaining sugar.

VARIATION

For a Nectarine and Apricot Tart with Almond Cream, replace the peaches with nectarines, prepared and arranged the same way. Peel and chop three fresh apricots. Fill the spaces between the fanned-out nectarines with chopped apricots. Bake as above.

Raspberry Tart

This glazed fruit tart really does taste as good as it looks.

INGREDIENTS

Serves 8

4 egg yolks

65g/2½ oz/⅓ cup granulated sugar

45ml/3 tbsp plain flour

300ml/½ pint/1¼ cups milk

pinch of salt

2.5ml/½ tsp vanilla essence

450g/1lb fresh raspberries

75ml/5 tbsp grape or redcurrant jelly

15ml/1 tbsp fresh orange juice

For the pastry

150g/5oz/1¼ cups plain flour

2.5ml/½ tsp baking powder

1.5ml/¼ tsp salt

15ml/1 tbsp sugar

grated rind of ½ orange

90ml/6 tbsp cold butter, cut in pieces

1 egg yolk

45–60ml/3–4 tbsp whipping cream

1 For the pastry, sift the flour, baking powder and salt into a bowl. Stir in the sugar and orange rind. Add the butter and mix until the mixture resembles coarse crumbs. With a fork, stir in the egg yolk and just enough cream to bind the dough. Gather into a ball, wrap in greaseproof paper and chill.

2 For the custard filling, beat the egg yolks and sugar until thick and lemon-coloured. Gradually stir in the flour.

3 In a saucepan, bring the milk and salt just to the boil, and remove from the heat. Whisk into the egg yolk mixture, return to the pan, and continue whisking over moderately high heat until just bubbling. Cook for 3 minutes to thicken. Transfer immediately to a bowl. Stir in the vanilla to blend.

4 Cover with greaseproof paper to prevent a skin from forming.

5 Preheat the oven to 200°C/ 400°F/Gas 6. On a lightly floured surface, roll out the dough about 3mm/⅛in thick, transfer to a 25cm/10in flan tin and trim the edge. Prick the bottom all over with a fork and line with greaseproof paper. Fill with baking beans and bake for 15 minutes. Remove the paper and baking beans. Continue baking until golden, 6–8 minutes more. Let cool.

6 Spread an even layer of the pastry cream filling in the tart shell and arrange the raspberries on top. Melt the jelly and orange juice in a pan over a low heat and brush on top to glaze.

Kiwi Ricotta Cheese Tart

*It is well worth taking your time
arranging the kiwi fruit topping in
neat rows for this exotic and
impressive-looking tart.*

INGREDIENTS

Serves 8

50g/2oz/½ cup blanched almonds

90g/3½oz/½ cup plus 15ml/1 tbsp
  caster sugar

900g/2lb/4 cups ricotta cheese

250ml/8fl oz/1 cup whipping cream

1 egg

3 egg yolks

15ml/1 tbsp plain flour

pinch of salt

30ml/2 tbsp rum

grated rind of 1 lemon

40ml/2½ tbsp lemon juice

50ml/2fl oz/¼ cup clear honey

5 kiwi fruit

For the pastry

150g/5oz/1¼ cups plain flour

15ml/1 tbsp granulated sugar

2.5ml/½ tsp salt

2.5ml/½ tsp baking powder

75g/3oz/6 tbsp cold butter, cut in pieces

1 egg yolk

45–60ml/3–4 tbsp whipping cream

1 For the pastry, sift the flour,
sugar, salt and baking powder
into a bowl. Cut in the butter until
the mixture resembles coarse
crumbs. Mix the egg yolk and
cream. Stir in just enough to bind
the dough.

2 Transfer to a lightly floured
surface, flatten slightly, wrap
in greaseproof paper and chill for
30 minutes. Preheat the oven to
220°C/425°F/Gas 7.

3 On a lightly floured surface,
roll out the dough 3mm/⅛in
thick and transfer to a 23cm/9in
springform tin. Crimp the edge.

4 Prick the bottom of the dough
all over with a fork. Line with
greaseproof paper and fill with
baking beans. Bake for 10 minutes.
Remove the paper and beans and
bake until golden, 6–8 minutes
more. Let cool. Reduce the heat to
180°C/350°F/Gas 4.

5 Grind the almonds finely with
15ml/1 tbsp of the sugar in a
food processor or blender.

6 With an electric mixer, beat
the ricotta until creamy. Add
the cream, egg, yolks, remaining
sugar, flour, salt, rum, lemon rind
and 30ml/2 tbsp of the lemon
juice. Beat to combine.

7 Stir in the ground almonds
until well blended.

8 Pour into the shell and bake
until golden, about 1 hour. Let
cool, then chill, loosely covered, for
2–3 hours. Unmould and place on
a serving plate.

9 Combine the honey and
remaining lemon juice for the
glaze. Set aside.

10 Peel the kiwis. Halve them
lengthwise, then cut
crosswise into 5mm/¼in slices.
Arrange the slices in rows across
the top of the tart. Just before
serving, brush with the glaze.

Lemon and Orange Tart

Refreshing citrus fruits in a crisp, nutty pastry case.

INGREDIENTS

Serves 8–10

115g/4oz/1 cup plain flour, sifted

115g/4oz/1 cup wholemeal flour

25g/1oz/3 tbsp ground hazelnuts

25g/1oz/3 tbsp icing sugar, sifted

pinch of salt

115g/4oz/½ cup unsalted butter

60ml/4 tbsp lemon curd

300ml/½ pint/1¼ cups whipped cream or
    fromage frais

4 oranges, peeled and thinly sliced

1 Place the flours, hazelnuts, sugar, salt and butter in a food processor and process in short bursts until the mixture resembles breadcrumbs. Add 30–45ml/ 2–3 tbsp cold water and process until the dough comes together.

2 Turn out on to a lightly floured surface and knead gently until smooth. Roll out and line a 25cm/10in flan tin. Ease the pastry gently into the corners without stretching it. Chill for 20 minutes. Preheat the oven to 190°C/375°F/Gas 5.

3 Line the pastry with grease-proof paper and fill with baking beans. Bake blind for 15 minutes, remove the paper and beans and continue for a further 5–10 minutes, until the pastry is crisp. Allow to cool.

4 Whisk the lemon curd into the cream or fromage frais and spread over the base of the pastry. Arrange the orange slices on top and serve at room temperature.

Chocolate Pear Tart

Serve slices of this drizzled with single cream or with a scoop of vanilla ice cream for a special treat.

Serves 8

115g/4oz plain chocolate, grated
3 large firm, ripe pears
1 egg
1 egg yolk
120ml/4fl oz/½ cup single cream
2.5ml/½ tsp vanilla essence
45ml/3 tbsp caster sugar

For the pastry
115g/4oz/1 cup plain flour
pinch of salt
30ml/2 tbsp caster sugar
115g/4oz/½ cup cold unsalted butter, cut into pieces
1 egg yolk
15ml/1 tbsp fresh lemon juice

1 For the pastry, sift the flour and salt into a bowl. Add the sugar and butter. Cut in with a pastry blender until the mixture resembles coarse crumbs. With a fork, stir in the egg yolk and lemon juice until the mixture forms a dough. Gather into a ball, wrap in greaseproof paper, and chill for at least 20 minutes.

2 Place a baking sheet in the oven and preheat to 200°C/400°F/Gas 6. On a lightly floured surface, roll out the dough to 3mm/⅛in thick and trim the edge. Transfer to a 25cm/10in flan tin.

3 Sprinkle the bottom of the tart shell with the grated chocolate.

4 Peel, halve and core the pears. Cut in thin slices crosswise, then fan them out slightly.

5 Transfer the pear halves to the tart with the help of a metal spatula and arrange on top of the chocolate to resemble the spokes of a wheel.

6 Whisk together the egg and egg yolk, cream and vanilla essence. Ladle over the pears, then sprinkle with sugar.

7 Bake for 10 minutes. Reduce the heat to 180°C/350°F/Gas 4 and cook until the custard is set and the pears begin to caramelize, about 20 minutes more. Serve at room temperature.

Blueberry-Hazelnut Cheesecake

The base for this cheesecake is made with ground hazelnuts – a tasty and unusual alternative to a biscuit base.

INGREDIENTS

Serves 6–8

350g/12oz blueberries

15ml/1 tbsp clear honey

75g/3oz/6 tbsp granulated sugar

juice of 1 lemon

175g/6oz/¾ cup cream cheese, at room temperature

1 egg

5ml/1 tsp hazelnut liqueur (optional)

120ml/4fl oz/½ cup whipping cream

For the base

175g/6oz/1⅔ cups ground hazelnuts

75g/3oz/⅔ cup plain flour

pinch of salt

50g/2oz/4 tbsp butter, at room temperature

65g/2½oz/⅓ cup light brown sugar, firmly packed

1 egg yolk

1 For the base, put the hazelnuts in a large bowl. Sift in the flour and salt, and stir to mix. Set aside.

2 Beat the butter with the brown sugar until light and fluffy. Beat in the egg yolk. Gradually fold in the nut mixture, in three batches, until well combined.

3 Press the dough into a greased 23cm/9in pie tin, spreading it evenly against the sides. Form a rim around the top edge that is slightly thicker than the sides. Cover and chill for at least 30 minutes.

4 Preheat the oven to 180°C/350°F/Gas 4. Meanwhile, for the topping, combine the blueberries, honey, 15ml/1 tbsp of the granulated sugar and 5ml/1 tsp lemon juice in a heavy saucepan. Cook the mixture over low heat, stirring occasionally, until the berries have given off some liquid but still retain their shape, 5–7 minutes. Remove from the heat and set aside.

5 Place the pastry base in the oven and bake for 15 minutes. Remove and let cool while making the filling.

6 Beat together the cream cheese and remaining granulated sugar until light and fluffy. Add the egg, 15ml/1 tbsp lemon juice, the liqueur, if using, and the cream and beat until thoroughly blended.

7 Pour the cheese mixture into the pastry base and spread evenly. Bake until just set, 20–25 minutes.

8 Let the cheesecake cool completely on a wire rack, then cover and chill for at least 1 hour.

9 Spread the blueberry mixture evenly over the top of the cheesecake. Serve at cool room temperature.

COOK'S TIP

The cheesecake can be prepared 1 day in advance, but add the fruit shortly before serving.

Raspberry and White Chocolate Cheesecake

Raspberries and white chocolate are an irresistible combination, especially when teamed with rich mascarpone on a crunchy ginger and pecan nut base.

INGREDIENTS

Serves 8

50g/2oz/4 tbsp unsalted butter

225g/8oz/2⅓ cups ginger nut biscuits, crushed

50g/2oz/½ cup chopped pecan nuts or walnuts

For the filling

275g/10oz/1¼ cups mascarpone cheese

175g/6oz/¾ cup fromage frais

2 eggs, beaten

45ml/3 tbsp caster sugar

250g/9oz white chocolate, broken into squares

225g/8oz/1⅓ cups fresh or frozen raspberries

For the topping

115g/4oz/½ cup mascarpone cheese

75g/3oz/⅓ cup fromage frais

white chocolate curls and raspberries, to decorate

1 Preheat the oven to 150°C/ 300°F/Gas 2. Melt the butter in a saucepan, then stir in the crushed biscuits and nuts. Press into the base of a 23cm/9in spring-form cake tin.

2 Make the filling. Beat the mascarpone and fromage frais in a bowl, then beat in the eggs and caster sugar until evenly mixed.

3 Melt the white chocolate gently in a heatproof bowl over hot water.

4 Stir the chocolate into the cheese mixture with the raspberries.

5 Tip into the prepared tin and spread evenly, then bake for about 1 hour or until just set. Switch off the oven, but do not remove the cheesecake. Leave it until cold and completely set.

6 Release the tin and lift the cheesecake on to a plate. Make the topping by mixing the mascarpone and fromage frais in a bowl and spread over the cheesecake. Decorate with chocolate curls and raspberries.

Treacle Tart

*Quite a filling tart, this, so best
served after a light main course.*

INGREDIENTS

Serves 4–6
175ml/6fl oz/¾ cup golden syrup
75g/3oz/1½ cups fresh white breadcrumbs
grated rind of 1 lemon
30ml/2 tbsp fresh lemon juice

For the pastry
150g/5oz/1¼ cups flour
2.5ml/½ tsp salt
75g/3oz/6 tbsp cold butter, cut in pieces
75g/3oz/3 tbsp cold margarine, cut
   in pieces

1 For the pastry, combine the
flour and salt in a bowl. Add
the butter and margarine and cut
in with a pastry blender until the
mixture resembles coarse crumbs.

2 With a fork, stir in just enough
iced water (about 45–60ml/
3–4 tbsp) to bind the dough.
Gather into a ball, wrap in greaseproof paper, and chill for at least
20 minutes.

3 On a lightly floured surface,
roll out the dough 3mm/⅛in
thick. Transfer to a 20cm/8in flan
tin and trim off the overhang.
Chill for at least 20 minutes.
Reserve the trimmings for the
lattice top.

4 Place a baking sheet above the
centre of the oven and heat to
200°C/400°F/Gas 6.

5 In a saucepan, warm the syrup
until thin and runny.

6 Remove from the heat and stir
in the breadcrumbs and
lemon rind. Let sit for 10 minutes
so the bread can absorb the syrup.
Add more breadcrumbs if the
mixture is thin. Stir in the lemon
juice and spread evenly in the
pastry shell.

7 Roll out the pastry trimmings
and cut into 10–12 thin strips.

8 Lay half the strips on the
filling, then carefully arrange
the remaining strips to form a
lattice pattern.

9 Place on the hot sheet and
bake for 10 minutes. Lower
the heat to 190°C/375°F/Gas 5.
Bake until golden, about 15
minutes more. Serve warm or cold.

Rich Chocolate-Berry Tart

*Use any berries you like to top this
exotic tart.*

INGREDIENTS

Serves 10

115g/4oz/½ cup unsalted butter, softened

90g/3½oz/½ cup caster sugar

2.5ml/½ tsp salt

15ml/1 tbsp vanilla essence

50g/2oz/½ cup unsweetened cocoa

215g/7½oz/1¾ cups plain flour

450g/1lb fresh berries for topping

For the chocolate ganache filling

475ml/16fl oz/2 cups double cream

150g/5oz/½ cup seedless blackberry
    preserve

225g/8oz plain chocolate, chopped

25g/1oz/2 tbsp unsalted butter

For the blackberry sauce

225g/8oz fresh or frozen blackberries
    or raspberries

15ml/1 tbsp lemon juice

25g/1oz/2 tbsp caster sugar

30ml/2 tbsp blackberry liqueur

1 Prepare the pastry. Place the
butter, sugar, salt and vanilla in
a food processor and process until
creamy. Add the cocoa and process
for 1 minute. Add the flour all at
once and process for 10–15
seconds, until just blended. Place a
piece of clear film on a work
surface. Turn out the dough on to
the clear film. Use the film to help
shape the dough into a flat disc
and wrap tightly. Chill for 1 hour.

2 Lightly grease a 23cm/9in tart
tin with a removable base. Roll
out the dough between two sheets
of clear film to a 28cm/11in round,
about 5 mm/¼in thick. Peel off the
top sheet of clear film and invert
the dough into the prepared tin.
Ease it in. Remove the clear film.

3 With floured fingers, press the
dough on to the base and sides
of the tin, then roll a rolling pin
over the edge of the tin to cut off
any excess dough. Prick the base
with a fork. Chill for 1 hour.
Preheat the oven to 180°C/
350°F/Gas 4. Line the tart with foil
or baking paper; fill with dry
beans. Bake for 10 minutes; lift out
the foil with the beans and bake for
5 minutes more, until just set
(pastry may look underdone on
the bottom, but will dry out).
Remove to a wire rack to cool.

4 Prepare the filling. In a
medium saucepan over
medium heat, bring the cream and
blackberry preserve to the boil.
Remove from the heat and add the
chocolate, stirring until smooth.
Stir in the butter and strain into
the cooled tart, smoothing the top.
Cool the tart completely.

5 Prepare the sauce. In a food
processor combine the blackberries, lemon juice and sugar and
process until smooth. Strain into a
bowl and add the liqueur. If it is
too thick, thin with a little water.

6 To serve, remove the tart from
the tin. Place on a serving
plate and arrange the berries on
top. With a pastry brush, brush
with a little of the blackberry sauce
to glaze lightly. Serve the
remaining sauce separately.

Bakewell Tart

Although the pastry base makes this a tart, the original recipe describes it as a pudding.

INGREDIENTS

Serves 4

225g/8oz ready-made puff pastry

30ml/2 tbsp raspberry or apricot jam

2 eggs

2 egg yolks

115g/4oz/generous ½ cup caster sugar

115g/4oz/½ cup butter, melted

50g/2oz/½ cup ground almonds

few drops of almond essence

icing sugar, for sifting

1 Preheat the oven to 200°C/
400°F/Gas 6. Roll out the pastry on a lightly floured surface and use it to line an 18cm/7in pie plate or loose-based flan tin. Spread the jam over the bottom of the pastry case.

COOK'S TIP

Since this pastry case isn't baked blind first, place a baking sheet in the oven while it preheats, then place the flan tin on the hot sheet. This will ensure that the bottom of the pastry case cooks right through.

2 Whisk the eggs, egg yolks and sugar together in a large bowl until thick and pale.

3 Gently stir the butter, ground almonds and almond essence into the mixture.

4 Pour the mixture into the pastry case and bake for 30 minutes, until the filling is just set and browned. Sift icing sugar over the top before serving the tart hot, warm or cold.

VARIATION

Ground hazelnuts are increasingly available and make an interesting change to the almonds in this tart. If you are going to grind shelled hazelnuts yourself, first roast them in the oven for 10–15 minutes to bring out their flavour then rub in a dish towel to remove skins.

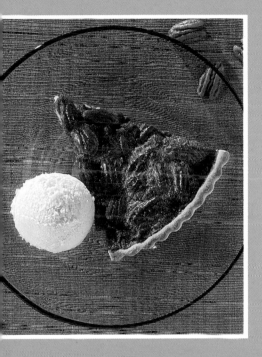

INTERNATIONAL CLASSICS

~

Apple Pie

Delicious on its own, or with a dollop of double cream or ice cream.

INGREDIENTS

Serves 8
900g/2lb tart cooking apples
30ml/2 tbsp plain flour
90g/3½oz/½ cup sugar
25ml/1½ tbsp fresh lemon juice
2.5ml/½ tsp ground cinnamon
2.5ml/½ tsp ground allspice
1.5ml/¼ tsp ground ginger
1.5ml/¼ tsp grated nutmeg
1.5ml/¼ tsp salt
50g/2oz/4 tbsp butter, diced

For the pastry
225g/8oz/2 cups plain flour
5ml/1 tsp salt
75g/3oz/6 tbsp cold butter, cut into pieces
50g/2oz/4 tbsp cold lard, cut into pieces

1 For the pastry, sift the flour and salt into a bowl.

2 Add the butter and lard and cut in with a pastry blender or rub between your fingertips until the mixture resembles coarse crumbs. With a fork, stir in just enough iced water to bind the dough (60–120ml/4–8 tbsp).

3 Gather into two balls, wrap in greaseproof paper and chill for 20 minutes.

4 On a lightly floured surface, roll out one dough ball to 3mm/⅛in thick. Transfer to a 23cm/9in pie tin and trim the edge. Place a baking sheet in the centre of the oven and preheat to 220°C/425°F/Gas 7.

5 Peel, core and slice the apples into a bowl. Toss with the flour, sugar, lemon juice, spices and salt. Spoon into the pie shell and dot with butter.

6 Roll out the remaining dough. Place on top of the pie and trim to leave a 2cm/¾in overhang. Fold the overhang under the bottom dough and press to seal. Crimp the edge.

7 Roll out the scraps and cut out leaf shapes and roll balls for the holly decoration. Arrange on top of the pie. Cut steam vents.

8 Bake for 10 minutes. Reduce the heat to 180°C/350°F/Gas 4 and bake until golden, 40–45 minutes more. If the pie browns too quickly, protect with foil.

Apple Brown Betty

This simple dessert tastes good with cream or ice cream.

Serves 6

50g/2oz/1 cup fresh breadcrumbs

50g/2oz/¾ cup light brown sugar, firmly packed

2.5ml/½ tsp ground cinnamon

1.5ml/¼ tsp ground cloves

1.5ml/¼ tsp grated nutmeg

50g/2oz/4 tbsp butter

900g/2lb tart-sweet apples

juice of 1 lemon

50g/2oz/⅓ cup finely chopped walnuts

1 Preheat the grill. Spread the breadcrumbs on a baking sheet and toast under the grill until golden, stirring so they colour evenly. Set aside.

2 Preheat the oven to 190°C/375°F/Gas 5. Butter a 2.4 litre/4 pint/2 quart baking dish. Set aside.

3 Mix the sugar with the spices. Cut the butter into pea-size pieces. Set aside.

4 Peel, core and slice the apples. Toss immediately with the lemon juice to prevent the apple slices from turning brown.

5 Sprinkle about 40ml/2½ tbsp of breadcrumbs over the bottom of the prepared dish. Cover with a third of the apple slices and sprinkle with a third of the sugar-spice mixture. Add another layer of breadcrumbs and dot with a third of the butter. Repeat the layers two more times, ending with a layer of bread-crumbs. Sprinkle with the nuts, and dot with the remaining butter.

6 Bake until the apples are tender and the top is golden brown, 35–40 minutes. Serve warm or cold.

American Spiced Pumpkin Pie

The unofficial national dish of the United States.

Serves 4–6

175g/6oz/1½ cups plain flour

pinch of salt

75g/3oz/6 tbsp unsalted butter

15ml/1 tbsp caster sugar

450g/1lb/4 cups peeled fresh pumpkin, cubed, or 400g/14oz/2 cups canned pumpkin, drained

115g/4oz/½ cup soft light brown sugar

1.5ml/¼ tsp salt

1.5ml/¼ ground allspice

2.5ml/½ tsp ground cinnamon

2.5ml/½ tsp ground ginger

2 eggs, lightly beaten

120ml/4fl oz/½ cup double cream

whipped cream, to serve

1 Place the flour in a bowl with the salt and butter and rub with your fingertips until the mixture resembles breadcrumbs (or use a food processor).

2 Stir in the sugar and add about 30-45ml/2-3 tbsp water and mix to a soft dough. Knead the dough lightly on a floured surface. Flatten out into a round, wrap in a polythene bag and chill for 1 hour.

3 Preheat the oven to 200°C/400°F/Gas 6 with a baking sheet inside. If you are using raw pumpkin for the pie, steam for 15 minutes until quite tender, then leave to cool completely. Purée the steamed or canned pumpkin in a food processor or blender until it is very smooth.

4 Roll out the pastry quite thinly and use to line a 24cm/9½in (measured across the top) x 2.5cm/1in deep pie tin. Trim off any excess pastry and reserve for the decoration. Prick the base of the pastry case with a fork.

5 Cut as many leaf shapes as you can from the excess pastry and make vein markings with the back of a knife on each. Brush the edge of the pastry with water and stick the leaves all round the edge. Chill.

6 In a large bowl mix together the pumpkin purée, sugar, salt, spices, eggs and cream and pour into the prepared pastry case. Smooth the top with a knife.

7 Place on the preheated baking sheet and bake for 15 minutes. Then reduce the temperature to 180°C/350°F/Gas 4 and cook for a further 30 minutes, or until the filling is set and the pastry golden. Serve the pie warm with a generous dollop of whipped cream.

Mississippi Pecan Pie

This fabulous dessert started life in the United States but has become an international favourite.

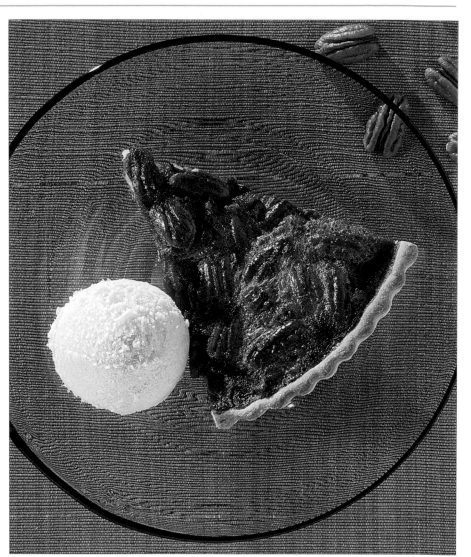

INGREDIENTS

Serves 6–8

For the pastry

115g/4oz/1 cup plain flour

50g/2oz/4 tbsp butter, cubed

25g/1oz/2 tbsp caster sugar

1 egg yolk

For the filling

175g/6oz/½ cup golden syrup

50g/2oz/⅓ cup dark muscovado sugar

50g/2oz/4 tbsp butter

3 eggs, lightly beaten

2.5ml/½ tsp vanilla essence

150g/5oz/1¼ cups pecan nuts

fresh cream or ice cream, to serve

1 Place the flour in a bowl and add the butter. Rub in the butter with your fingertips until the mixture resembles bread-crumbs, then stir in the sugar, egg yolk and about 30ml/2 tbsp cold water. Mix to a dough and knead lightly on a floured surface until smooth.

2 Roll out the pastry and use to line a 20cm/8in loose-based fluted flan tin. Prick the base, then line with greaseproof paper and fill with baking beans. Chill for 30 minutes. Preheat the oven to 200°C/400°F/Gas 6.

3 Bake the pastry case for 10 minutes. Remove the paper and beans and bake for 5 minutes. Reduce the oven temperature to 180°C/350°F/Gas 4.

4 Meanwhile, heat the syrup, sugar and butter in a pan until the sugar dissolves. Remove from the heat and cool slightly. Whisk in the eggs and vanilla essence and stir in the pecans.

5 Pour into the pastry case and bake for 35–40 minutes, until the filling is set. Serve with cream or ice cream.

Boston Banoffee Pie

There are many variations of this American treat; this one is easy to make and tastes wonderful.

INGREDIENTS

Serves 6–8

150g/5oz/1¼ cups plain flour

225g/8oz/1 cup butter

50g/2oz/4 tbsp caster sugar

½ x 405g/14oz can skimmed, sweetened condensed milk

115g/4oz/⅔ cup soft light brown sugar

30ml/2 tbsp golden syrup

2 small bananas, sliced

a little lemon juice

whipped cream, to decorate

5ml/1 tsp grated plain chocolate

1 Preheat the oven to 160°C/ 325°F/Gas 3. Place the flour and 115g/4oz/½ cup of the butter in a food processor and blend until crumbed (or rub in with your fingertips). Stir in the caster sugar.

2 Squeeze the mixture together until it forms a dough. Press into the base of a 20cm/8in loose-based fluted flan tin. Bake for 25–30 minutes.

3 Place the remaining butter with the condensed milk, brown sugar and golden syrup in a large non-stick saucepan and heat gently, stirring, until the butter has melted and the sugar has dissolved.

4 Bring to a gentle boil and cook for 7 minutes, stirring all the time (to prevent burning), until the mixture thickens and turns a light caramel colour. Pour on to the cooked pastry base and leave until cold.

5 Sprinkle the bananas with lemon juice and arrange in overlapping circles on top of the caramel filling, leaving a gap in the centre. Pipe a swirl of whipped cream in the centre and sprinkle with the grated chocolate.

Vermont Baked Maple Custard

Try to find pure maple syrup for this custard as it will really enhance the flavour.

INGREDIENTS

Serves 6

3 eggs

120ml/4fl oz/½ cup maple syrup

600ml/1 pint/2½ cups milk

pinch of salt

pinch of grated nutmeg

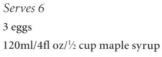

COOK'S TIP

Baking delicate mixtures such as custards in a water bath helps protect them from uneven heating which could make them rubbery.

1 Preheat the oven to 180°C/ 350°F/Gas 4. Combine all the ingredients in a large bowl and mix together thoroughly.

2 Set individual custard cups or ramekins in a roasting tin half filled with hot water. Pour the custard mixture into the cups. Bake until the custards are set, 45 minutes–1 hour. Test by inserting the blade of a knife in the centre: it should come out clean. Serve warm or chilled.

Crème Caramel

Crème caramel, or crème renversée, is one of the most popular French desserts and is wonderful when freshly made. This is a slightly lighter modern version of the traditional recipe.

INGREDIENTS

Serves 6–8

250g/9oz/1¼ cups granulated sugar

60ml/4 tbsp water

1 vanilla pod or 10ml/2 tsp vanilla essence

400ml/14fl oz/1⅔ cups milk

250ml/8fl oz/1 cup whipping cream

5 large eggs

2 egg yolks

1 Put 175g/6oz/⅞ cup of the sugar in a small heavy saucepan with 60ml/4 tbsp of water to moisten. Bring to the boil over a high heat, swirling the pan to dissolve the sugar. Boil, without stirring, until the syrup turns a dark caramel colour (this will take about 4–5 minutes).

2 Immediately pour the caramel into a 1 litre/1¾ pint/4 cup soufflé dish. Quickly swirl the dish to coat the base and sides with the caramel and set aside. (The caramel will harden quickly as it cools.) Place the dish in a small roasting tin.

3 Preheat the oven to 160°C/325°F/Gas 3. With a small sharp knife, carefully split the vanilla pod lengthways and scrape the black seeds into a medium saucepan, or add the vanilla essence. Add the milk and cream and bring just to the boil over a medium-high heat, stirring frequently. Remove the pan from the heat, cover and set aside for 15–20 minutes.

4 In a bowl, whisk the eggs and egg yolks with the remaining sugar for 2–3 minutes until smooth and creamy. Whisk in the hot milk and carefully strain the mixture into the caramel-lined dish. Cover with foil.

5 Place the dish in a roasting tin and pour in enough boiling water to come halfway up the sides of the dish. Bake the custard for 40–45 minutes until just set and a knife inserted about 5cm/2in from the edge comes out clean. Remove from the roasting tin and cool for at least 30 minutes, then chill overnight.

6 To turn out, carefully run a sharp knife round the edge of the dish to loosen the custard. Cover the dish with a serving plate and, holding them tightly, invert the dish and plate together. Gently lift one edge of the dish, allowing the caramel to run over the sides, then slowly lift off the dish.

Floating Islands

Originally these oval-shaped meringues were poached in milk and this was then used to make the rich custard sauce.

INGREDIENTS

Serves 4–6
1 vanilla pod
600ml/1 pint/2½ cups milk
8 egg yolks
50g/2oz/¼ cup granulated sugar

For the meringues
4 large egg whites
1.5ml/¼ tsp cream of tartar
225g/8oz/1¼ cups caster sugar

For the caramel
150g/5oz/¾ cup granulated sugar

1 Split the vanilla pod lengthways and scrape the seeds into a saucepan. Add the milk and bring just to the boil over a medium heat, stirring frequently. Cover and set aside for 15–20 minutes.

2 In a medium bowl, whisk the egg yolks and sugar for 2–3 minutes until thick and creamy. Whisk in the hot milk and return the mixture to the saucepan. With a wooden spoon, stir over a medium-low heat until the sauce begins to thicken and coat the back of the spoon (do not allow to boil). Immediately strain into a chilled bowl, allow to cool, stirring occasionally and then chill.

3 Half-fill a large wide frying pan or saucepan with water and bring just to simmering point. In a clean, grease-free bowl, whisk the egg whites until frothy. Add the cream of tartar and continue whisking until they form soft peaks. Sprinkle over the caster sugar, about 30ml/2 tbsp at a time, and whisk until the whites are stiff and glossy.

4 Using two tablespoons, form egg-shaped meringues and slide them into the water (you may need to work in batches). Poach them for 2–3 minutes, turning once until just firm. Using a large slotted spoon, transfer the cooked meringues to a baking sheet lined with kitchen paper to drain.

5 Pour the cold custard into individual serving dishes and arrange the meringues on top.

6 To make the caramel, put the sugar into a small saucepan with 45ml/3 tbsp of water to moisten. Bring to the boil over a high heat, swirling the pan to dissolve the sugar. Boil, without stirring, until the syrup turns a dark caramel colour. Immediately drizzle the caramel over the meringues and custard in a zig-zag pattern. Serve cold. (The caramel will soften if made too far ahead.)

Crème Brûlée

This dessert actually originated in Cambridge, but has become associated with France and is widely eaten there. Add a little liqueur, if you like, but it is equally delicious without it.

Serves 6

1 vanilla pod

1 litre/1¾ pints/4 cups double cream

6 egg yolks

90g/3½oz/½ cup caster sugar

30ml/2 tbsp almond or orange liqueur
  (optional)

75g/3oz/⅓ cup soft light brown sugar

1 Preheat the oven to 150°C/300°F/Gas 2. Place six 120ml/4fl oz/½ cup ramekins in a roasting tin and set aside.

2 With a small sharp knife, split the vanilla pod lengthways and scrape the black seeds into a medium saucepan. Add the cream and bring just to the boil over a medium heat, stirring. Remove from the heat and cover. Set aside for 15–20 minutes.

COOK'S TIP

To test if the custards are ready, push the point of a knife into the centre of one – if it comes out clean, the custards are cooked.

3 In a bowl, whisk the egg yolks, caster sugar and liqueur, if using, until well blended. Whisk in the hot cream and strain into a large jug. Divide the custard equally among the ramekins.

4 Pour enough boiling water into the roasting tin to come halfway up the sides of the ramekins. Cover the tin with foil and bake for about 30 minutes until the custards are just set. Remove from the tin and leave to cool. Return to the dry roasting tin and chill.

5 Preheat the grill. Sprinkle the sugar evenly over the surface of each custard and grill for 30–60 seconds until the sugar melts and caramelizes. (Do not let the sugar burn or the custard curdle.) Place in the fridge to set the crust and chill completely before serving.

Tarte au Citron

You can find this classic lemon tart in bistros all over France.

INGREDIENTS

Serves 8–10

350g/12oz shortcrust or sweet shortcrust pastry

grated rind of 2 or 3 lemons

150ml/¼ pint/⅔ cup freshly squeezed lemon juice

90g/3½oz/½ cup caster sugar

60ml/4 tbsp crème fraîche or double cream

4 eggs, plus 3 egg yolks

icing sugar, for dusting

1 Preheat the oven to 190°C/375°F/Gas 5. Roll out the pastry thinly and use to line a 23cm/9in flan tin. Prick the base of the pastry.

2 Line the pastry case with foil and fill with baking beans. Bake for about 15 minutes until the edges are set and dry. Remove the foil and beans and continue baking for a further 5–7 minutes until golden.

3 Place the lemon rind, juice and sugar in a bowl. Beat until combined and then gradually add the crème fraîche or double cream and beat until well blended.

4 Beat in the eggs, one at a time, then beat in the egg yolks and pour the filling into the pastry case. Bake for 15–20 minutes, until the filling is set. If the pastry begins to brown too much, cover the edges with foil. Leave to cool. Dust with a little icing sugar before serving.

Pear and Almond Cream Tart

This tart is equally successful made with other kinds of fruit, and some variation can be seen in almost every good French pâtisserie. Try making it with nectarines, peaches, apricots or apples.

INGREDIENTS

Serves 6

350g/12oz shortcrust or sweet shortcrust
    pastry
3 firm pears
lemon juice
15ml/1 tbsp peach brandy or water
60ml/4 tbsp peach preserve, strained

For the almond cream filling
115g/4oz/¾ cup blanched whole almonds
50g/2oz/¼ cup caster sugar
65g/2½oz/5 tbsp butter
1 egg, plus 1 egg white
few drops almond essence

1 Roll out the pastry thinly and use to line a 23cm/9in flan tin. Chill the pastry case while you make the filling. Put the almonds and sugar in a food processor and pulse until finely ground; they should not be pasty. Add the butter and process until creamy, then add the egg, egg white and almond essence and mix well.

2 Place a baking sheet in the oven and preheat to 190°C/375°F/Gas 5. Peel the pears, halve them, remove the cores and rub with lemon juice.

3 Put the pear halves cut-side down on a board and slice thinly crossways, keeping the slices together.

4 Pour the almond cream filling into the pastry case. Slide a palette knife under one pear half and press the top with your fingers to fan out the slices. Transfer to the tart, placing the fruit on the filling like spokes of a wheel. If you like, remove a few slices from each half before arranging and use to fill in any gaps in the centre.

5 Place on the baking sheet and bake for 50–55 minutes until the filling is set and well browned. Cool on a rack.

6 Meanwhile, heat the brandy or water and the preserve in a small saucepan, then brush over the top of the hot tart to glaze. Serve the tart warm, at room temperature.

Greek Chocolate Mousse Tartlets

The combination of white chocolate and Greek-style yogurt makes an irresistibly light, but not too sweet, filling.

INGREDIENTS

Serves 6

175g/6oz/1½ cups plain flour
30ml/2 tbsp cocoa powder
30ml/2 tbsp icing sugar
115g/4oz/½ cup butter
melted dark chocolate, to decorate

For the filling

200g/7oz white chocolate, broken into
    squares
120ml/4fl oz/½ cup milk
10ml/2 tsp powdered gelatine
30ml/2 tbsp caster sugar
5ml/1 tsp vanilla essence
2 eggs, separated
250g/9oz/generous 1 cup Greek-style
    yogurt

1 Preheat the oven to 190°C/ 375°F/Gas 5. Sift the flour, cocoa and icing sugar into a large bowl.

2 Place the butter in a pan with 60ml/4 tbsp water and heat gently until just melted. Cool, then stir into the flour to make a smooth dough. Chill until firm.

3 Roll out the pastry and line six deep 10cm/4in loose-based flan tins.

4 Prick the base of each pastry case all over with a fork, cover with greaseproof paper weighted down with baking beans and bake blind for 10 minutes. Remove the baking beans and paper, return to the oven and bake a further 15 minutes or until the pastry is firm. Leave to cool in the tins.

5 Make the filling. Melt the chocolate in a heatproof bowl over hot water. Pour the milk into a saucepan, sprinkle over the gelatine and heat gently, stirring, until the gelatine has dissolved completely. Remove from the heat and stir in the chocolate.

6 Whisk the sugar, vanilla essence and egg yolks in a large bowl, then beat in the chocolate mixture. Beat in the yogurt until evenly mixed.

7 Whisk the egg whites in a clean, grease-free bowl until stiff, then fold into the mixture. Divide among the pastry cases and leave to set.

8 Drizzle the melted dark chocolate over the tartlets to decorate.

Chestnut Pudding

This is an Italian speciality, made during the months of October and November, when fresh sweet chestnuts are gathered.

INGREDIENTS

Serves 4–5

450g/1lb fresh sweet chestnuts

300ml/½ pint/1¼ cups milk

115g/4oz/½ cup caster sugar

2 eggs, separated, at room temperature

25g/1oz/¼ cup unsweetened
   cocoa powder

2.5ml/½ tsp pure vanilla essence

50g/2oz/½ cup icing sugar, sifted

fresh whipped cream, to garnish

marrons glacés, to garnish

1 Cut a cross in the side of the chestnuts, and drop them into a pan of boiling water. Cook for 5–6 minutes. Remove with a slotted spoon, and peel while still warm.

2 Place the peeled chestnuts in a heavy or non-stick saucepan with the milk and half of the caster sugar. Cook over low heat, stirring occasionally, until soft. Remove from the heat and allow to cool. Press the contents of the pan through a strainer.

3 Preheat the oven to 180°C/ 350°F/Gas 4. Beat the egg yolks with the remaining caster sugar until the mixture is pale yellow and fluffy. Beat in the cocoa powder and the vanilla.

4 In a separate bowl, whisk the egg whites with a wire whisk or electric beater until they form soft peaks. Gradually beat in the sifted icing sugar and continue beating until the mixture forms stiff peaks.

5 Fold the chestnut and egg yolk mixtures together. Fold in the egg whites. Turn the mixture into one large or several individual buttered pudding moulds. Place on a baking sheet, and bake in the oven for 12–20 minutes, depending on the size. Remove from the oven, and allow to cool for 10 minutes before unmould- ing. Serve garnished with whipped cream and marrons glacés.

Coffee Granita

A granita is a cross between a frozen drink and a flavoured ice, very popular in Italy. The consistency should be slushy, not solid. They can be made at home with the help of a food processor.

INGREDIENTS

Serves 4–5

115g/4oz/½ cup granulated sugar
250ml/8fl oz/1 cup very strong espresso coffee, cooled
whipped cream, to garnish (optional)

1 Heat 475ml/16fl oz/2 cups of water with the sugar over low heat until the sugar dissolves. Bring to the boil. Remove from the heat and allow to cool.

2 Combine the coffee with the sugar syrup. Place in a shallow container or freezer tray, and freeze until solid. Plunge the bottom of the frozen container or tray in very hot water for a few seconds. Turn the frozen mixture out, and chop it into large chunks.

3 Place the mixture in a food processor fitted with a metal blade, and process until it forms small crystals. Spoon into serving glasses and top with whipped cream, if desired. If you do not wish to serve the granita immediately, pour the processed mixture back into a shallow container or ice tray and freeze until serving time. Allow to thaw for a few minutes before serving, or process again.

Lemon Granita

Nothing is more refreshing on a hot summer's day than a cooling lemon granita.

INGREDIENTS

Serves 4–5

115g/4oz/½ cup granulated sugar
grated rind of 1 lemon, scrubbed before grating
juice of 2 large lemons

1 Heat 475ml/16fl oz/2 cups of water with the sugar over low heat until the sugar dissolves. Bring to the boil. Remove from the heat, and allow to cool.

2 Combine the lemon rind and juice with the sugar syrup. Place in a shallow container or freezer tray, and freeze until solid.

3 Plunge the bottom of the frozen container or tray in very hot water for a few seconds. Turn the frozen mixture out, and chop it into chunks.

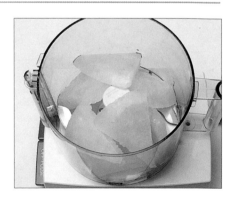

4 Place the mixture in a food processor fitted with a metal blade, and process until it forms small crystals. Spoon into individual serving glasses.

Peach Melba

The story goes that one of the great French chefs, Auguste Escoffier, created this dessert in honour of the opera singer Nellie Melba, now forever enshrined in culinary, if not musical, history.

INGREDIENTS

Serves 6

50g/2oz/¼ cup caster sugar

1 vanilla pod, split lengthways

3 large peaches

For the sauce

450g/1lb/2⅔ cups fresh or frozen
   raspberries

15ml/1 tbsp lemon juice

25–40g/1–1½oz/2–3 tbsp caster sugar

30–45ml/2–3 tbsp raspberry liqueur
   (optional)

vanilla ice cream, to serve

mint leaves and fresh raspberries, to
   decorate (optional)

1 In a saucepan large enough to hold the peach halves in a single layer, combine 1 litre/ 1¾ pints/4 cups of water with the sugar and vanilla pod. Bring to the boil over a medium heat, stirring occasionally to dissolve the sugar.

2 Cut the peaches in half and twist the halves to separate them. Using a small teaspoon, remove the peach stones. Add the peach halves to the poaching syrup, cut-sides down, adding more water, if needed, to cover the fruit. Press a piece of greaseproof paper against the surface, reduce the heat to medium-low, then cover and simmer for 12–15 minutes until tender – the time will depend on the ripeness of the fruit. Remove the pan from the heat and leave the peaches to cool in the syrup.

3 Remove the peaches from the syrup and peel off the skins. Place on several thicknesses of kitchen paper to drain (reserve the syrup for another use), then cover and chill.

4 Put the raspberries, lemon juice and sugar in a blender or food processor fitted with the metal blade. Process for 1 minute, scraping down the sides once. Press through a fine sieve into a small bowl, then stir in the raspberry liqueur, if using, and put in the fridge to chill.

5 To serve, place a peach half, cut-side up, on a dessert plate, fill with a scoop of vanilla ice cream and spoon the raspberry sauce over the ice cream. Decorate with mint leaves and a few fresh raspberries, if using.

Australian Hazelnut Pavlova

Meringue topped with fresh fruit and cream – perfect for summer dinner parties.

INGREDIENTS

Serves 4–6

3 egg whites

175g/6oz/generous ¾ cup caster sugar

5ml/1 tsp cornflour

5ml/1 tsp white wine vinegar

40g/1½oz/5 tbsp chopped roasted
    hazelnuts

250ml/8fl oz/1 cup double cream

15ml/1 tbsp orange juice

30ml/2 tbsp natural thick and creamy
    yogurt

2 ripe nectarines, stoned and sliced

225g/8oz/1⅓ cups raspberries

15–30ml/1–2 tbsp redcurrant jelly,
    warmed

1 Preheat the oven to
140°C/275°F/Gas 1. Lightly
grease a baking sheet. Draw a
20cm/8in circle on a sheet of
baking parchment. Place pencil-
side down on the baking sheet.

2 Place the egg whites in a clean,
grease-free bowl and whisk
with an electric mixer until stiff.
Whisk in the sugar 15ml/1 tbsp at
a time, whisking well after each
addition.

3 Add the cornflour, vinegar and
hazelnuts and fold in carefully
with a large metal spoon.

4 Spoon the meringue on to the
marked circle and spread out,
making a dip in the centre.

5 Bake for about 1¼–1½ hours,
until crisp. Leave to cool, then
transfer to a serving platter.

6 Whip the cream and orange
juice until just thick, stir in the
yogurt and spoon on to the
meringue. Top with the fruit and
drizzle over the redcurrant jelly.
Serve immediately.

Lemon Ricotta Cake

This lemony cake from Sardinia is quite different from a traditional cheesecake.

INGREDIENTS

Serves 6–8

75g/3oz/6 tbsp butter

175g/6oz/¾ cup granulated sugar

75g/3oz/generous ⅓ cup ricotta cheese

3 eggs, separated

175g/6oz/1½ cups plain flour

grated rind of 1 lemon

45ml/3 tbsp fresh lemon juice

7.5ml/1½ tsp baking powder

icing sugar, for dusting

1 Grease a 23cm/9in round cake or springform tin. Line the bottom with baking parchment or greaseproof paper. Grease the paper. Dust with flour. Set aside. Preheat the oven to 180°C/350°F/Gas 4.

2 Cream the butter and sugar together until smooth. Beat in the ricotta cheese.

3 Beat in the egg yolks, one at a time. Add 30ml/2 tbsp of the flour, and the lemon rind and juice. Sift the baking powder into the remaining flour and beat into the batter until well blended only.

4 Beat the egg whites until they form stiff peaks. Fold them carefully into the batter.

5 Turn the mixture into the prepared tin. Bake for 45 minutes, or until a cake tester inserted in the centre of the cake comes out clean. Allow the cake to cool for 10 minutes before turning it out on to a rack to cool. Dust the cake generously with icing sugar before serving.

Peaches with Amaretti Stuffing

Peaches are plentiful all over Italy. They are sometimes prepared hot, as in this classic dish.

INGREDIENTS

Serves 4

4 ripe fresh peaches

juice of ½ lemon

65g/2½oz/⅔ cup amaretti biscuits, crushed

30ml/2 tbsp marsala, brandy or peach brandy

25g/1oz/2 tbsp butter, at room temperature

2.5ml/½ tsp vanilla essence

30ml/2 tbsp granulated sugar

1 egg yolk

1 Preheat the oven to 180°C/350°F/Gas 4. Wash the peaches. Cut them in half and remove the stones. Enlarge the hollow left by the stones by scooping out some of the peach with a small spoon. Sprinkle the peach halves with the lemon juice.

2 Soften the amaretti crumbs in the marsala or brandy for a few minutes. Beat the butter until soft. Stir in the amaretti mixture and all the remaining ingredients.

3 Arrange the peach halves in a baking dish in one layer hollow side upwards. Divide the amaretti mixture into 8 parts, and fill the hollows, mounding the stuffing up in the centre. Bake for 35–40 minutes. These are delicious served hot or cold.

Bread Pudding with Pecan Nuts

A version of the British classic deliciously flavoured with pecan nuts and orange rind.

INGREDIENTS

Serves 6

400ml/14fl oz/1⅔ cups milk

400ml/14fl oz/1⅔ cups single or whipping
   cream

150g/5oz/¾ cup caster sugar

3 eggs, beaten to mix

10ml/2 tsp grated orange rind

5ml/1 tsp vanilla essence

24 slices of day-old French bread,
   1.5cm/½in thick

75g/3oz/½ cup toasted pecan nuts,
   chopped

icing sugar, for sprinkling

whipped cream or soured cream and
   maple syrup, to serve

1 Put 350ml/12fl oz/1½ cups each of the milk and cream in a saucepan. Add the sugar. Warm over low heat, stirring to dissolve the sugar. Remove from the heat and cool. Add the eggs, orange rind and vanilla and mix well.

2 Arrange half of the bread slices in a buttered 23–25cm/9–10in baking dish. Scatter two-thirds of the pecans over the bread. Arrange the remaining bread slices on top and scatter on the rest of the pecans.

3 Pour the egg mixture evenly over the bread slices. Soak for 30 minutes. Press the top layer of bread down into the liquid once or twice.

4 Preheat the oven to 180°C/350°F/Gas 4. If the top layer of bread slices looks dry and all the liquid has been absorbed, moisten with the remaining milk and cream.

5 Set the baking dish in a roasting tin. Add enough water to the tin to come halfway up the sides of the dish. Bring the water to the boil.

6 Transfer to the oven. Bake for 40 minutes or until the pudding is set and golden brown on top. Sprinkle the top of the pudding with sifted icing sugar and serve warm, with whipped cream or soured cream and maple syrup, if you like.

Spiced Peach Crumble

The topping of this classic dessert has rolled oats added for extra crunchiness.

Serves 6

1.5kg/3lb ripe but firm peaches, peeled, stoned and sliced
60ml/4 tbsp caster sugar
2.5ml/½ tsp ground cinnamon
5ml/1 tsp lemon juice
whipped cream or vanilla ice cream, for serving (optional)

For the topping

115g/4oz/1 cup plain flour
1.5ml/¼ tsp ground cinnamon
1.5ml/¼ tsp ground allspice
75g/3oz/1 cup rolled oats
175g/6oz/¾ cup soft light brown sugar
115g/4oz/8 tbsp butter

1 Preheat the oven to 190°C/375°F/Gas 5. For the topping, sift the flour and spices into a bowl. Add the oats and sugar and stir to combine. Cut or rub in the butter until the mixture resembles coarse crumbs.

2 Toss the peaches with the sugar, cinnamon and lemon juice. Put the fruit mixture in a 20–23cm/8–9in diameter baking dish.

3 Scatter the topping over the fruit in an even layer. Bake for 30–35 minutes. Serve warm, with whipped cream or vanilla ice cream, if liked.

VARIATION

Use apricots or nectarines instead of peaches. Substitute nutmeg for the cinnamon.

Jam Tart

Jam tarts are popular in Italy where they are traditionally decorated with pastry strips.

INGREDIENTS

Serves 6–8

200g/7oz/1¾ cups plain flour

pinch of salt

50g/2oz/¼ cup granulated sugar

115g/4oz/½ cup butter or margarine, chilled

1 egg

1.5ml/¼ tsp grated lemon rind

350g/12oz/1¼ cups fruit jam, such as raspberry, apricot or strawberry

1 egg, lightly beaten with 30ml/2 tbsp whipping cream, for glazing

1 Make the pastry by placing the flour, salt and sugar in a mixing bowl. Using a pastry blender or two knives, cut the butter or margarine into the dry ingredients as quickly as possible until the mixture resembles coarse crumbs.

2 Beat the egg with the lemon rind in a cup and pour it over the flour mixture. Combine with a fork until the dough holds together. If it is too crumbly, mix in 15–30ml/1–2 tbsp of water.

3 Gather the dough into two balls, one slightly larger than the other, and flatten into discs. Wrap in greaseproof or waxed paper and put in the fridge for at least 40 minutes.

4 Lightly grease a shallow 23cm/9in tart or pie tin, preferably with a removable bottom. Roll out the larger disc of pastry on a lightly floured surface to a thickness of about 3mm/⅛in.

5 Roll the pastry round the rolling pin and transfer to the prepared tin. Trim the edges evenly with a small knife. Prick the bottom with a fork. Chill for at least 30 minutes.

6 Preheat the oven to 190°C/ 375°F/Gas 5. Spread the jam thickly and evenly over the base of the pastry. Roll out the remaining pastry.

7 Cut the pastry into strips about 1cm/½in wide using a ruler as a guide. Arrange them over the jam in a lattice pattern. Trim the edges of the strips even with the edge of the tin, pressing them lightly on to the pastry shell. Brush the pastry with the egg and cream glaze. Bake for about 35 minutes or until the pastry is golden brown. Allow to cool before serving.

Indian Ice Cream (Kulfi)

Kulfi-wallahs (ice cream vendors) have always made kulfi, and continue to this day, without using modern freezers. Try this method – it works extremely well in an ordinary freezer. You will need to start making kulfi the day before you want to serve it.

INGREDIENTS

Serves 4–6

3 x 400ml/14fl oz cans evaporated milk

3 egg whites, whisked until peaks form

350g/12oz/3 cups icing sugar

5ml/1 tsp cardamom powder

15ml/1 tbsp rose water

175g/6oz/1½ cups pistachios, chopped

75g/3oz/generous ½ cup sultanas

75g/3oz/¾ cup sliced almonds

25g/1oz/2 tbsp glacé cherries, halved

1 Remove the labels from the cans of evaporated milk and lay the cans down in a pan with a tight-fitting cover. Fill the pan with water to reach three-quarters up the cans. Bring to the boil, cover and simmer for 20 minutes. When cool, remove and chill the cans in the fridge for 24 hours.

2 Open the cans and empty the milk into a large, chilled bowl. Whisk until it doubles in quantity, then fold in the whisked egg whites and icing sugar.

3 Gently fold in the remaining ingredients, seal the bowl with cling film and leave in the freezer for 1 hour.

4 Remove the ice cream from the freezer and mix well with a fork. Transfer to a freezer container and return to the freezer for a final setting. Remove from the freezer 10 minutes before serving in scoops.

Spiced Mexican Fritters

Hot, sweet and spicy fritters are popular in both Spain and Mexico for either breakfast or a snack.

INGREDIENTS

Makes 16 (serves 4)
175g/6oz/1 cup raspberries
45ml/3 tbsp icing sugar
45ml/3 tbsp orange juice

For the fritters
50g/2oz/4 tbsp butter
65g/2½oz/⅔ cup plain flour, sifted
2 eggs, lightly beaten
15ml/1 tbsp ground almonds
corn oil, for frying
15ml/1 tbsp icing sugar and 2.5ml/½ tsp
   ground cinnamon, for dusting
8 fresh raspberries, to decorate

1 Mash the raspberries with the icing sugar, push through a sieve into a bowl to remove all the seeds. Stir in the orange juice and chill until ready to serve.

2 To make the fritters, place the butter and 150ml/¼ pint/ ⅔ cup water in a saucepan and heat gently until the butter has melted. Bring to the boil and, when boiling, add the sifted flour all at once and turn off the heat.

3 Beat until the mixture leaves the sides of the pan and forms a ball. Cool slightly then beat in the eggs a little at a time, then add the almonds.

4 Spoon the mixture into a piping bag fitted with a large star nozzle. Half-fill a saucepan or deep-fat fryer with the oil and heat to 190°C/375°F.

5 Pipe about four 5cm/2in lengths at a time into the hot oil, cutting off the raw mixture with a knife as you go. Deep-fry for about 3–4 minutes, turning occasionally, until puffed up and golden. Drain on kitchen paper and keep warm in the oven while frying the remainder.

6 When you have fried all the mixture, dust the hot fritters with icing sugar and cinnamon. Serve three or four per person on serving plates drizzled with a little of the raspberry sauce, dust again with sieved icing sugar and decorate with fresh raspberries.

Thai Fried Bananas

A very simple and quick Thai pudding – bananas fried in butter, brown sugar and lime juice, and sprinkled with toasted coconut.

INGREDIENTS

Serves 4
40g/1½oz/3 tbsp butter
4 large slightly under-ripe bananas
15ml/1 tbsp desiccated coconut
60ml/4 tbsp soft light brown sugar
60ml/4 tbsp lime juice
2 fresh lime slices, to decorate
thick and creamy natural yogurt, to serve

1 Heat the butter in a large frying pan or wok and fry the bananas for 1–2 minutes on each side, or until they are lightly golden in colour.

2 Meanwhile, dry-fry the coconut in a small frying pan until lightly browned, and reserve.

3 Sprinkle the sugar into the pan with the bananas, add the lime juice and cook, stirring until dissolved. Arrange bananas on a serving dish. Sprinkle the coconut over the bananas, decorate with lime slices and serve with the thick and creamy yogurt.

Index